God Box

Unleashing the Freedom and Wholeness of the Holy Spirit

Heather V. Shore

God Box: Unleashing the Freedom and Wholeness of the Holy Spirit
By Heather V. Shore
Sun Creek Press
Evergreen, CO 80439
© 2022 Heather V. Shore

All rights reserved. Printed in the United States of America. No part of this publication may be reproduced, stored in a retrieval system or transmitted in any form or by any means, electronic, mechanical, photocopying, recording or otherwise, without the written permission of the publisher.

Cover design by Roy Roper, wideyedesign.

ISBN 978-0-578-35890-1

All Scripture quotations, unless otherwise indicated, are taken from the Holy Bible, New International Version®, NIV®. Copyright © 1973, 1978, 1984, 2011 by Biblica, Inc.™ Used by permission of Zondervan. All rights reserved worldwide, www.zondervan.com. The "NIV" and "New International Version" are trademarks registered in the United States Patent and Trademark office by Biblica, Inc.™

Scripture quotations marked (AMP) taken from the Amplified® Bible, Copyright © 2015 by The Lockman Foundation. Used by permission. www.Lockman.org.

Scripture quotations marked CSB have been taken from the Christian Standard Bible®, Copyright © 2017 by Holman Bible Publishers. Used by permission. Christian Standard Bible® and CSB® are federally registered trademarks of Holman Bible Publishers.

Scripture marked (ERV) are taken from the HOLY BIBLE: EASY-TO-READ VERSION © 2014 by Bible League International. Used by permission.

Scripture quotations marked (ESV) are from The Holy Bible, English Standard Version® (ESV®), copyright © 2001 by Crossway, a publishing ministry of Good News Publishers. Used by permission. All rights reserved.

Scriptures and additional materials quoted and marked (GNT) are from the Good News Bible © 1994 published by the Bible Societies/HarperCollins Publishers Ltd UK, Good News Bible© American Bible Society 1966, 1971, 1976, 1992. Used with permission.

Scriptures marked ISV are taken from the International Standard Version (ISV), copyright© 1996-2008 by the ISV Foundation. All rights reserved internationally.

Scripture quotations from the King James Version (KJV), public domain.

Scripture taken from the Modern English Version (MEV). Copyright © 2014 by Military Bible Association. Used by permission. All rights reserved.

Scripture quotations marked (NASB) or (NASB1995) taken from the New American Standard Bible®, Copyright © 1960, 1962, 1963, 1968, 1971, 1972, 1973, 1975, 1977, 1995 by The Lockman Foundation. Used by permission. All rights reserved. www.Lockman.org.

Scripture taken from the New King James Version® (NKJV). Copyright © 1982 by Thomas Nelson. Used by permission. All rights reserved.

Scripture quotations marked (NLT) are taken from the Holy Bible, New Living Translation, copyright ©1996, 2004, 2007, 2013 by Tyndale House Foundation. Used by permission of Tyndale House Publishers, Inc., Carol Stream, Illinois 60188. All rights reserved.

Scripture marked (TLV) taken from the Holy Scriptures, Tree of Life Version. Copyright © 2014,2016 by the Tree of Life Bible Society. Used by permission of the Tree of Life Bible Society.

Scripture quotations marked (TPT) are from The Passion Translation®. Copyright © 2017, 2018 by Passion & Fire Ministries, Inc. Used by permission. All rights reserved. ThePassionTranslation.com.

The World English Bible (WEB) is in the Public Domain.

Set your eyes on Him and run your race. Faith is the daring of the soul to go further than it can see. What journey could be greater?

But seek first the kingdom of God and his righteousness, and all these things will be added to you.

—

Matthew 6:33 (ESV)

Contents

Foreword

Introduction

Chapter 1: Finding Freedom and Wholeness in Faith

Chapter 2: Finding Freedom and Wholeness in Identity

Chapter 3: Finding Freedom and Wholeness from Self-Contempt and Self-Abuse

Chapter 4: Finding Freedom and Wholeness in Health

Chapter 5: Finding Freedom and Wholeness in Relationships

Chapter 6: Finding Freedom and Wholeness in Financial Decisions

Chapter 7: Finding Freedom and Wholeness in Parenting

Chapter 8: Finding Freedom and Wholeness in Choices through Wisdom

Chapter 9: Finding Freedom and Wholeness from Religious and Poverty Spirits

Chapter 10: Finding Freedom and Wholeness in Abundance through Surrender

Appendix

Foreword

The book you're now holding in your hands was written by my dear friend Heather Shore. I first met Heather just over two years ago, when we were connected through a mutual friend who sensed that the healing journeys, we were each pursuing might provide a source of strength and encouragement to both of us. She was right. Though Heather and I each had very different experiences, we both found ourselves in similar places, feeling lost, empty, and hopeless.

As a Christ follower, it can be disorienting realizing that you are unable to draw on the faith and hope that had always come so easily in the past. This book is Heather's gift to the body of Christ. It is a record of what she learned as she chose to look beyond her circumstances and determined to devote herself to discovering God for who he is, not for who she had limited him to be. This project was born out of a difficult journey that resulted in a broken heart and spirit, which led to a surrendered and laid-down life that brought the kind of freedom only God can bring.

Having shared a similar experience, I can personally attest to the supernatural power and life-changing revelations Heather recounts as she encountered Papa God, Holy Spirit, and King Jesus in spirit and truth. This same reality is available to all of us who have confessed faith in Christ. You don't have to settle for a life of less than or good enough. Scripture tells us that Jesus came to give us life to the full! Unfortunately, we often fail to grasp the possibility that Christ died to provide for us because our finite minds struggle with this reality. Heather explains how she discovered, and embraced, this truth and how it changed everything.

Today Heather has a remarkable testimony of God's faithfulness, and this book is evidence of that gift. I had the privilege of walking much of that path with her, and now you're able to do the same. My prayer is that, like Heather, you will have the courage to open your heart and mind to receive all that God is waiting to give you, as you follow her lead to a surrendered and fully abundant life.

Blessings,

Tina Hansen

Introduction

I put God in a box. A pretty, blue, large box. Full of compartments where he could only oversee certain parts at certain times. You get the gist: i.e., he oversees the budget this month, or he's in charge of my attitude this week. Very compartmentalized and on my terms.

Somewhere along the way this box mentality started to shift. God showed up in 2017 and started to reshape my box. To the point where there is no longer a box at all. I took him out of the box and let him be in charge. Of. It. All.

How do you do that, you ask? Well, I finally got my head screwed on straight. Just kidding. In reality, I finally came to the end of myself. I was so tired of living in a state of perpetual motion, performance, and striving for acceptance that I gave up. Gave up in a good way. When you run into a prophet at Subway who tells you Matthew 6:33 (NLT)— "Seek the Kingdom of God above all else, and life righteously, and he will give you everything you need"—you listen. God is telling you, "Hey, pay attention. If you follow me, watch out, because it is going to be crazy fun. But you have to let me out of the box."

Throughout this book we are going to talk about finding freedom and wholeness through the Holy Spirit. What does it look like, how do you practically apply what God reveals to you, and how do you live this out? At the end of each chapter will be a little section of questions called "Unleash the Box." Those questions will help make you think, make you ask God important questions, and hopefully encourage you to receive life-changing truths. My hope is for everyone who reads these words to come to know Him. Truly know Father, Jesus, and Holy Spirit in ways only he can show you. So buckle up. It is going to be a fun ride. The ride of a lifetime.

Prayer: As we pray your will be done, we do so knowing the answer will be the Holy Spirit, who will come and further the agenda that God has in our lives. You, our God, are a loving Father who delights in giving what is best to your children, which is why we can pray with confidence knowing that you hear our prayers. In Jesus's name, amen.

Chapter 1: Finding Freedom and Wholeness in Faith

What if surrendering to God is the way to freedom? What if in the surrender we find out not only the purpose to our life, but how to take God out of a box and allow the adventure to begin? It's through the ultimate life surrender we not only become free, but we also become whole. In wholeness we become ourselves. To live free, we need to give up our right to understand.

—Jenna Winston

My journey to finding freedom and wholeness came through sitting on the back side of the mountain. Literally and figuratively. I live in the mountains of Colorado. It is beautiful, breathtaking, and awe-inspiring regarding creation. It can also be an isolating, lonely, and hard place at times. What people do not realize about Colorado is that the independent spirit of the people seeps into every area of the culture. This independent spirit can lead to times of questioning, seeking your own way, and trying to find wholeness in things which are not life-giving. That is until God puts you on the back side of the mountain and says, "Sit, heal, and listen." You see, American culture has become so independence seeking, we have forgotten there is a big God wanting to have a big relationship with us. We have put God in a box. He is tucked away on a shelf wanting to be let down and walk alongside us in the journey. How come we have put him away? Because we do not understand what it truly means to be free and whole. Let us discover how to be free and whole in our faith and many other areas of life.

Finding Freedom

Finding freedom is a topic near to my heart. Freedom is something I've always craved in order to live life my way. But I eventually realized my way was not getting me too far and keeping God in a box wasn't serving me well either. So many people long to be free and have an abundant life. What if there is a different way to gain freedom and wholeness?

What Is Freedom?

What is freedom? Freedom, in the simplest terms, is the state of being unencumbered instead of imprisoned or enslaved. It is the right to act, speak, or think as one wants without hindrance or restraint. Living in freedom means living without the struggles that keep us imprisoned or continually making choices that hinder our lives. The goal is to move forward in different areas that might keep us down.

What is abundant living? Abundant living is the call to fullness of life. "I have come that they may have life, and that they may have it more abundantly" (John 10:10 NKJV). "More abundantly means to have a superabundance of a thing. 'Abundant life' refers to life in its abounding fullness of joy and strength for mind, body, and soul."[1] This abundant life signifies a contrast of feelings of lack, emptiness, and dissatisfaction, and motivates us to seek and change our life.

As we walk through trials that change our lives, we should contemplate what questions can help us attain freedom, such as "How is this trial shaping my life and others around me?" During times of hope and joy, we may ask more questions about abundant living, such as, "How can I live with more joy?" Regardless of the season we're in, when the shaping of our soul occurs, freedom becomes important because it helps us respond to what is before us.

Freedom Journey

What does freedom and wholeness have to do with our journeys? Everything.

The choices I've made inside and outside the will of God continue to affect my overall life situation. Ultimately, my goal is improved health—spiritual, emotional, and physical. I want what Stormie Omartian defined in *Lord, I Want to Be Whole*: "My definition of emotional health is having total peace with who you are, what you're doing, and where you're going, both individually and in relationship to those around you. It is feeling totally at peace about the past, present, and future of your life. It's knowing that you're in line with God's ultimate purpose for you and being fulfilled in that. When you have that kind of peace and you no longer live in emotional agony, then you are a success."[2] This means learning about abundant living in Christ and how to walk forward in freedom. Only through Father God can anyone find true freedom.

Why go into this discussion on freedom? As my journey continues to unfold, freedom is becoming the central focus of my life. I have found freedom in Christ fundamental to growing, living with hope, and advancing in life. Freedom and wholeness truly do unlock the key to an abundant life, and it is something we are called to as followers. My hope for others is to understand there is freedom waiting for them. It can happen. Choose God.

The Back Side of the Mountain

Sometimes, freedom and wholeness come from a season of forced quietness. I recently met with a dear friend, and we caught up on our lives. She wanted to get together and hear how life was going. This trustworthy person kept saying this phrase, which I had never heard before: "You're on the back side of the mountain." She explained that I have been strategically placed in solitude to prepare me for the work of God. The back side can also be a place of transition and pruning. Those are words I have fought against while trying to find freedom, but I have come to realize these quiet times are needed to become whole.

What Does the Back Side of the Mountain Look Like?

It is a quiet place. It's a place where we are grown, groomed, and loved. We sometimes must sit there for years and other times for a short while. How long you sit there depends on how much of the world needs to be removed from you. I love this definition of the back side from Michael Jake's sermon: "Sometimes the Lord needs to remove us from what we know and expect to prepare us for a greater work. It's a strategic and obscure place where the Lord places us to prune us."[3] Those words finally excite me! The adjectives and verbs he uses to describe the back side give you an idea of what is intended by God. The back side involves refreshment, preparation, pruning, solitude, development, lowliness, growth, instruction, and transition. All those words lead to so much growth.

Another article I found in *Charisma Leader Magazine* stated it this way: "The paradox of the desert is that in the quiet dryness of the moment, thoughts often are unscrambled while priorities are reassembled. In the desert, God's voice can be clearly heard."[4] Only when we get quiet with no distractions can we hear God's voice. I personally want my priorities reassembled and unscrambled so I know how to navigate the desert, this season on the back side of the mountain.

How to Navigate the Back Side

The word confidence has been huge for me this year in which this book was published. Part of being in a season like this means having the confidence to understand where we are and be able to sit amid the back side well. Here is the deal: God will sometimes strip us of the things in our lives that tend to replace him, including our own self-sufficiency. This stripping happens on the back side, and as a result, the hope is that we find our confidence in him. God is love, and he does not violate his character. His judgment is always an expression of his love to bring us into conformity with him and his will for us. Navigating this season includes the stripping of self-sufficiency and allowing his confidence to fill us.

How Long Does It Last?

We do not have a clue how long the back side will last. Until everyone and everything is stripped away? Possibly. But in God's goodness and kindness, he will slowly place people and opportunities back into our life. In my life, he's been reminding me that I am not alone on the back side. We always have God. Whatever your season looks like, whether it is a growing and refreshing time or a time of being stripped and humbled, rest in knowing something great is coming around the corner. The back side doesn't last forever, but the sweetness that comes will enable you to live out your purpose.

Single-Mindedness versus Double-Mindedness

One piece of my faith walk over the past few years has been learning how my distorted thinking was affecting all my decisions. During my back-side season, God brought up my double-minded viewpoint as something needing to be healed and removed from my life. The desire to have a single-minded view of God's kingdom rather than my double-mindedness, where I was only pleasing my own interests, began to weigh heavily upon me. Not having the proper view of God's gracious gift to us really kept me bound in my old wounds and hurt. That was the enemy's plan—to keep me focused on the wrong things. In doing so, I was completely ineffective for his kingdom. The enemy's goal is to make us so caught up in the world's problems and issues, we completely forget to have an eternal perspective in our faith walk. Once God gets ahold of our minds and direction, his kingdom values become our values.

    Single-mindedness is being one-souled, meaning one life is being lived here, with God's life freely coming forth from one's heart and producing godly life actions! Examples of mighty faith warriors who had this view include Abraham, Isaac, and Joseph. In Genesis 39, Joseph was assigned to Potiphar's house as overseer because Potiphar trusted him completely. Potiphar committed everything into Joseph's hands, and God blessed Potiphar because of this.

    Potiphar's wife then did everything she could to get him to sleep with her. In retaliation when he wouldn't, she lied to Potiphar saying Joseph attacked her. Potiphar had to put Joseph in jail. But as Genesis 39:21 (MEV) explains, "The LORD was with Joseph and showed him mercy and gave him favor in the sight of the keeper of the prison." Everyone who saw Joseph saw God was with him.

David, however, was double-minded. According to 2 Samuel 11, when David saw Bathsheba, he had to have her, subsequently having her husband killed. Even though he had God's life in his heart and had been "a man after [God's] own heart" (1 Samuel 13:14 NIV), he nevertheless chose to go with the tide and follow the lusts of his own flesh over what God was prompting him to do (also see Acts 13:22). Every man is tempted by desire and evil (James 1:14–15), but David's words of "I love God" and his actions did not match. People could no longer see God in him. He had totally given himself over to his own will and desires, and thus, God's life was quenched in David's own heart and life.

Satan revels in our double-mindedness! He knows that double-mindedness not only keeps us bound, but it also causes the enemies of God to blaspheme. All Satan and his hordes want is to have us respond "emotionally," in other words, for our emotional choices to follow our hurts and pain. We are going to be either single-minded, allowing God's life to motivate us from our hearts and direct all our actions, or double-minded, blocking God's life in our hearts and showing only the "self life" in our soul.[5]

Being single-minded brings light to our lives, and we are also happier and more content when we focus on the kingdom of God and his righteousness, knowing all the material things will be added to us, i.e., taken care of, by our heavenly Father (Matthew 6:33). But when we are double-minded, it is as if our whole body is full of darkness. We try to live for two masters at the same time, and it puts a dark shadow over everything in our life.

We are to be concerned with the right things—the paramount issues of life—and we can then leave the management (and the worry) over material things with our heavenly Father. Our life is more important than those trivial matters, and we have eternal matters to pursue, after all. God provides for the birds and takes care of them (Matthew 6:26); birds do not worry, but they do work.

The worry many people have over the material things of life is rooted in a low understanding of their value before God. There are greater sins than worry, but there are none more self-defeating and useless. Worry can harm ourselves through stress. Instead, seeking first the kingdom of God must be the rule of our lives when ordering our priorities. In everything we do, we must seek first the kingdom of God.

Jesus reminds us that our physical well-being is not a worthy object to devote our lives to. Jesus did not just tell his followers to stop worrying; he told them to replace worry with a concern for the kingdom of God. A habit or passion. A commitment to find and to do the will of God, to ally oneself totally with his purpose. If you put God's kingdom first and do not think that your physical well-being is a worthy object to live your life for, you then may enjoy the life he gives back to you. He promises heavenly treasures, rest in divine provision, and fulfillment of God's highest purpose for man: fellowship with him and being part of his kingdom. Seeking first the kingdom of God is a fundamental choice everyone makes after they repent and are converted. Our Christian life will either reinforce that decision or deny it on a daily basis. In Matthew 6:34, God wants us to remember the past, plan for the future, but live in the present.

Freedom and wholeness are possible when we take our thoughts captive away from double-mindedness and give our thought lives over to his kingdom. Recognize the back side of the mountain as a place where we are to quiet ourselves before God and seek his kingdom, a place that will bring about the freedom and wholeness we all long for in our lives.

Scripture around Freedom in Faith

- Matthew 6:33 (ESV): "But seek first the kingdom of God and his righteousness, and all these things will be added to you."
- James 1:5–8 (NIV): "If any of you lacks wisdom, you should ask God, who gives generously to all without finding fault, and it will be given to you. But when you ask, you must believe and not doubt, because the one who doubts is like a wave of the sea, blown and tossed by the wind. That person should not expect to receive anything from the Lord. Such a person is double-minded and unstable in all they do."
- Lamentations 3:23 (ESV): "The steadfast love of the LORD never ceases; his mercies never come to an end; they are new every morning; great is your faithfulness."

- 2 Corinthians 5:7 (NIV): "For we live by faith, not by sight."
- Zechariah 4:10 (NLT): "Do not despise these small beginnings, for the LORD rejoices to see the work begin, to see the plumb line in Zerubbabel's hand."

Unleash the Box

1. What can you do to find freedom today in your life?
2. How will you become more single-minded? How can you end double-minded thinking?
3. What is one step you can take to navigate the back side of the mountain well?
4. How is the kindness of God tied into your freedom and wholeness journey?
5. Where are you allowing the world and your emotions to influence your thinking?
6. What is one tiny step of obedience you can take toward God in helping you find freedom and wholeness in faith?

Prayer: Papa God, we seek you first. No more constraints. We take you out of the box. In doing so, please reform our thinking and our attitudes and show us how to love you, ourselves, and others well. Only through your freedom can we come into right understanding of your kingdom and its ways. Let it be so with us. In Jesus's name, amen.

Chapter 2: Finding Freedom and Wholeness in Identity

> *"You were BORN TO BREAK THE BOX! You have looked down upon yourself for the fire within you, but I placed the anointing upon you and the fire within you to BREAK BOXES that man's wisdom and expectation have created. You were not born to live in a box. You were born to BREAK THE BOXES through the expression of My heart, My love and My fire through you. You are coming forth! You are coming forth My wild one! Bridled no longer! Free to run! Free to soar!"*
>
> —Lana Vawser

Our God desires truth in our innermost being (Psalm 51:6). This truth relates to who he created us to be in our identity. Our identity comes from knowing who we are in Christ and knowing without a shadow of a doubt who our Creator is. Our identity is pieced together in his creative way to show us not only the depth and height of his love, but also shows us his vast mercy, grace, and goodness to his people. When we accept Jesus as our Savior, we come into right relationship with the Father, the Son, and the Holy Spirit. The Trinity was created in relationship and desires to have a relationship with each one of us who chooses to have a relationship with them. Isn't it amazing the Creator of the universe desires for us to know him in relationship as Jesus knows him in relationship? Let us delve into how aligning our hearts with the Trinity can bring about such an identity shift that it allows us to experience freedom and wholeness.

Coming Into Right Relationship with the Trinity

Imagine yourself—you, your whole being—as a house. What would your house look like? How many doors and windows are part of your house? What does the outside look like? Is there a garden outside, landscaping or no landscaping, or a beautiful oasis that brings peace? What about the inside of your house—do you have a kitchen, a main living room, various bedrooms or other types of rooms, and is there any furniture? How does the layout of the house look? This exercise can help you delve into the foundation of what you believe. In the

Bible it calls our body a dwelling place, as in our house. The imagery of the house relates to the house's foundation, which is your inner being.

Our foundation, or inner being, needs to be based on the reality of the Bible and the truth of who God is. His truths that he shares in the Bible should be the building blocks for our foundation. What are the building blocks in your life? I have come to realize there is a process to understanding the building blocks that affect our relationship with the Trinity. When we lay down our lives and completely dismantle the existing framework (i.e., what we have believed about God and his truths found in the Bible), we come into a better understanding of the relationship the Father is seeking to have with us daily. If we really believe that the power of Jesus, which raised people from the dead, resides in us, how can we not lay down our lives and let God completely dismantle our framework of what we think is possible? The amazing truth is the power of Jesus lives in us! Romans 8:11 (NIV) says, "And if the Spirit of him who raised Jesus from the dead is living in you, he who raised Christ from the dead will also give life to your mortal bodies because of his Spirit who lives in you."

We walk in freedom and learn how to get free when we realize how God created us. God created us perfectly and wonderfully. He tears out the junk and provides restoration. He prunes the garden and gets the weeds out. During the pruning process, sort of a middle ground, is when the weeds come out and the true transformation begins of understanding our inheritance in Christ. Taking in all this gospel information does not bring about true transformation. Knowing your inheritance in God's kingdom is where the transforming mentality begins to shape your inner being. Do you truly take the mental assent and know Psalm 139 for yourself? For example, Psalm 139:13–14 (ESV) says, "For you formed my inward parts; you knitted me together in my mother's womb. I praise you, for I am fearfully and wonderfully made." This is your inheritance and identity in God's kingdom!

The thing is, God disciples us through life. He wants our restoration more than we do and always says yes to the restoration process in our lives. Isaiah talks a lot about the desolate inheritance and raising up and restoring the broken pathways. This restoration of our desolate places is a continual process leading us to know Father

God intimately. Father God is restoring and transforming us every day. Isaiah 58:12 (ESV) tells us, "And your ancient ruins shall be rebuilt; you shall raise up the foundations of many generations; you shall be called the repairer of the breach, the restorer of streets to dwell in." And Isaiah 49:11 (NIV) adds, "I will turn all my mountains into roads, and my highways will be raised up." Our broken pathways are the lies we have believed that have caused our brokenness; he restores and replaces those lies with his truth in our innermost being. He raises up our broken pathways, our brokenness, by restoring and sanctifying us so that we can come into right relationship with Papa God.

One time a friend said to me, "All of life is about relationship—all things are about right relationship with God." If this is true, how do we define right relationship with the Trinity and our identity? We learn to build our house upon the rock and recognize when the enemy, the father of lies, is knocking at our door. We start by building out the base framework upon Scripture. Our identity in Christ is discussed throughout Scripture, but some of my personal favorites include Psalm 139, Jeremiah 1:5 (NIV)—"Before I formed you in the womb, I knew you, before you were born, I set you apart; I appointed you as a prophet to the nations"—and 1 Peter 2:9 (NIV)—"But you are a chosen people, a royal priesthood, a holy nation, God's special possession, that you may declare the praises of him who called you out of darkness into his wonderful light."

We also add daily prayer and sitting and abiding with the Father into the mix. This creates the next level of framework in the house structure. Abiding builds the outer layer of protection around our foundation. Abiding is a lost art in our world today. Sitting in prayer with the Father and seeking to understand his heart for us is something we should all take the time to cultivate in our lives. Valuing God for who he is and pursuing spiritual intimacy with him is abiding. When you discover who he really is as Father, it will move you to discover who you truly are. This has been instrumental for me, causing me to learn not only my identity in Christ and how to build my house structure on his Word but also that his direction is possible with the help of the Father's hand. Seeking his input on all matters has helped me to cease striving and to grow as I've abided in him.

One thing the Western church has forgotten is that there is an enemy who is after us once we are a part of the royal priesthood. I am not saying fear him, but rather stand up to him. When we recognize we have a real enemy and have the blood of the Lamb above the door of our house, we allow the darkness to pass over us. Knowing we are God's, the enemy tries to take advantage and attack our house. John 10:10 (NIV) reminds us, "The thief comes only to steal and kill and destroy; I have come that they may have life and have it to the full." If we are to have life to the full, why do we let the enemy destroy our sense of our identity? How do we learn to take our thoughts captive instead of letting the enemy have a say in our lives? We are to *be* instead of *do*! So many of us *do* instead of *be*. We have his kingdom purposes wrong! He wants us to be okay in the *being* instead of *doing*. I had this wrong for so long. We go and go and go, until the point of exhaustion, thinking this is God's will. Not at all!

In the book of Matthew, Jesus talks about us having the yoke of his rest upon our being (Matthew 11:29). However, this is only possible through full surrender to his will for our lives. His yoke is easy and his burden is light *if* we claim the position he intends for us, not only in our identity but with the Holy Spirit within us. His position for us, our identity in him, involves coming into understanding of how he made us, how he views us, and how we are to rely on him for all things. When we rely on him for all things, he will never call us to do something we cannot handle or sustain. Our security, health, and whole being will be taken care of before he gives us any sort of platform, no matter the size. We must understand that no matter what is before us, no matter what he calls us to, we are to guard our hearts (Proverbs 4:23). We are to walk forward in our security, health, and whole being and live out our unique messages and calling from him. As long as we have light in our eyes, he is restoring life in us. As Psalms 51:12 (NIV) says, "Restore to me the joy of your salvation and grant me a willing spirit, to sustain me." What does this mean when it comes to our identity?

  The source of our identity empowers our choices. Parents encourage children to "remember who you are." How much more our Creator and Sustainer God, the Giver of Life, calls us to remember all people are made in His image with purpose, value, dignity, and worth. How we see others and ourselves matters. Authentic faith proves we are God's children. 2 So how do we pass on the importance of living out our identity in Christ? As my inner healing counselor, Kelly, once told me, we will always introduce the God we model. Are we living in victory and in the fullness of our inheritance in Christ? Or are we living from a spirit of poverty? An impoverished spirit is not accessing God's truth. Are we asking for rest, peace, and our true inheritance? We have a millionaire's inheritance, and yet most of us (including myself) have lived a pauper's existence.

Moving Out of Poverty and Into Inheritance

The religious and poverty spirits are alive and well in the Western church. The religious spirit is man-made effort that attempts to utilize works to please God. It is very easy to mistake being religious for having a relationship with God. [2] The religious spirit replaces our precious relationship with God with a lifestyle or attitude of good works over being with the Lord. The poverty spirit hinders believers in Christ. It is a state of feeling inferior, keeping you trapped in a lower state of being, which keeps you from living an ascended lifestyle. It keeps you from moving into the inheritance God promises. There are different types of poverty as well, such as poverty in imagination, in courage, and in self-image. Poverty keeps you from being all you are called to be and keeps you accepting limitations.

Poverty is a place of being governed by lack, where the lack itself governs you based on current resources at that time. It keeps you stagnant, not moving forward, not allowing you to step forward in faith to meet God's provision. When God gives you a promise, there is a process we must follow that will lead to provision. It is always a progression: promise, then process, then provision.

God's hope is for each of us to experience his promises in the land of the living. As Psalm 27:13–14 (NIV) proclaims, "I will see the goodness of the LORD *in the land of the living*! Wait for the LORD; be strong and take heart and wait for the LORD" (emphasis mine). This means moving out from under the poverty spirit and moving into our inheritance in the Lord. We, the children of God, those who belong to the Lord, are his heirs in Christ. His children are his heirs, as it says in James 2:5 (NASB1995): "Listen, my beloved brethren: did not God choose the poor of this world to be rich in faith and heirs of the kingdom which He promised to those who love Him?" What belongs to Jesus will also belong to us as joint heirs in the kingdom. Our inheritance involves many aspects. We will inherit our salvation, the kingdom of God, and even the whole earth. The Bible also speaks of glory, honor, and crowns in heaven. It will be an inheritance that is far grander than we could possibly imagine.[3]

Identity and inheritance in Christ are intrinsically tied together. You can't walk into your inheritance in Christ without fully understanding who you are in Christ. When we come out from under a religious or poverty mind-set or spirit and step into our identity in Christ, we welcome the inheritance set before us. As mentioned above in Psalm 27, our inheritance is what is awaiting us here on earth and in heaven. Will we receive crowns of glory or a pauper's welcome into the kingdom of God? We get to choose. We are free either to go boldly after our identity in Christ as sons or daughters or to choose to go our own way. When we choose to go after God's heart, what awaits us is a very exciting journey with him. He welcomes us, abides with us, and wants to walk us into our identity and inheritance in Him.

Scripture around Freedom in Identity

- Isaiah 43:1–2 (NIV): "But now, this is what the LORD says—he who created you, Jacob, he who formed you, Israel: 'Do not fear, for I have redeemed you; I have summoned you by name; you are mine. When you pass through the waters, I will be with you; and when you pass through the rivers, they will not sweep over you. When you walk through the fire, you will not be burned; the flames will not set you ablaze.'"

- Ephesians 2:10 (AMP): "For we are His workmanship [His own master work, a work of art], created in Christ Jesus [reborn from above—spiritually transformed, renewed, ready to be used] for good works, which God prepared [for us] beforehand [taking paths which He set], so that we would walk in them [living the good life which He prearranged and made ready for us]."

- 1 Peter 2:9 (NIV): "But you are a chosen people, a royal priesthood, a holy nation, God's special possession, that you may declare the praises of him who called you out of darkness into his wonderful light."

- 2 Corinthians 5:17 (ESV): "Therefore, if anyone is in Christ, he is a new creation. The old has passed away; behold, the new has come."

Unleash the Box

1. What limitations are you placing on God and yourself?
2. What are some ways can you partner with God on your identity and soak in the truth of who He says you are?
3. How would you describe the character of God? By knowing His character, you will know God.
4. Do you know the promises God speaks over you? What are some of your favorite promises found in the Bible? Understanding his promises helps to overcome the lies we believe and will bring us into our identity.
5. One exercise my inner healer counselor Kelly had us walk through is how our inner being is shaped through identifying it as a house. This exercise helps us to step into our identity is to

understand the framework of our inner being and where we have made partnerships (lies we have believed) with the enemy. A great way to delve into this is through understanding the makeup of your house. In the Bible it calls our body a dwelling place, as in our house. Our thought processes might represent the walls of our house. Ask the Holy Spirit to give you a picture of your body as a house. Is it big or small? Who is in our house? Who gets kicked out? How many windows are there? What is allowed in our house? How is it decorated? Are people there? Do you have neighbors, a yard? Is it rural or in a city? All these questions speak to our belief systems and paradigms. Ask God, "Where am I not giving voice to my current reality? Where am I stuffing or storing things and not expressing them?" This can create health issues. "What am I really feeling?" Be honest with God as you process everything in your life with him. He can handle it.

6. Attune your ears to your own prayers. Are you desperate? Begging? Confused on how to get God to move on your behalf or see your need? Confident? Hopeful? Excited? What do you

pray about? Needs? Desires? Circumstances? Changes in other people? Things you want fixed? List the things you are asking for, the things you're needing and believing for. Next to each prayer request, explain what scripture says about each item. Ask him to draw you into understanding of what is rightfully yours and all that belongs to you as his daughter or son.

7. Ask him for a Bible character to study. Read the story or verses associated with that character; then answer the following questions:

    A. What is true of the person of God and who he is in this story?

    B. What is true of the person in the story? What do I observe about him or her that is also available for anyone? Is there an invitation or a permission or a grace? What does God want me to know about the unchanging nature of who he is in the story that is also true of who he is to me or for me? How would God invite me to walk with him in the truths of this passage?

Prayer: I am made in God's image, empowered by God's spirit, and I am a part of God's plan. If my idea or dream is beyond my ability, God, you always provide a plan that is purposeful and perfect. I'm excited to see what you have in store. I hear you telling me, *If you show up, I'll show off. Open every door man would not. I have big dreams for you. Be filled with hope and the expectation of goodness. The less you control, the more I'll move!* Lord, help me respond. In Jesus's name, amen.

Chapter 3: Finding Freedom and Wholeness from Self-Contempt and Self-Abuse

Knowing that God is way bigger than anything we can imagine means we can release control. We can stop striving. And we can allow God to do what only He can. As Ephesians 3:20 tells us, God "is able to do immeasurably more than all we ask or imagine, according to his power that is at work within us."

—Leila Halawe

Sitting in the doctor's office wondering what weight I will be on the scale, I am concerned because they might call me obese. Being short in stature makes it hard not to be labeled obese. I am usually borderline on the weight curve, right in between normal and obese. What on earth does this have to do with self-contempt? Well, a few weeks ago, I was still abusing my body by doing cleanses and other nasty things to my body to hit a certain number on the scale. If I just hit that number, I will be okay, right? It will make me pretty, loved, and finally accepted by others. As you can tell from this twisted thinking, self-contempt is something I have personally struggled with for an exceptionally long time. Coming free from under this type of delusion has not been easy. Going through the house exercise in chapter 2 brought about freedom on this one issue right away during a recent inner healing session. Being raised without confidence and told how, when, and what to think can be detrimental to us later in life. Such was the case for me, I realized, as I sat in the doctor's office wondering what label they were going to give me. I hate labels, don't you?

Taking Away the Labels

As we come into agreement with what the Lord says about us as humans and see ourselves as he sees us, we can start to fully grasp and heal from the weight of self-abuse. For me, through lots of inner healing work and sessions with the Holy Spirit, these labels started to melt away. Anger, comparison, and control were replaced with God's love, peace, and provision. No longer were these the identity labels on me and how I related to the world, but they were released and gone from my house, i.e., my body.

The following revelation from Lana Vawser shows the Father's heart toward his daughters and how he wants to break us free from the roots of self-rejection:

> I am melting deep roots of self-hatred and bringing incredible restoration, release, recompense (making amends for loss and harm suffered) and restitution. Now My daughters will set into their destiny like never before and how I REJOICE over them with singing. I am inviting My daughters into a divine dance of intimacy with Me in the secret place that they have never experienced before. It will be like meeting Me for the first time all over again. The enemy has used the root of self-hatred for so long to keep My daughters bound, but no more, this is their day of RADICAL freedom and life-changing encounters with My love.

These encounters with My love uprooting the self-hatred in many are going to change the outlook, expression, and direction of many of My daughters. The uprooting this deep root will be a divine reference point for many of My daughters of where they stepped into a life-altering breakthrough and shift.

My daughters are arising in the revelation of My love like never before and these hidden places are being exposed, revealed, and healed as My daughters are about to run in the empowerment of My Spirit, passion, boldness and courage like never before. It is time! Their day of deliverance has arrived![1]

Vawser then quotes Ephesians 3:16–19 (AMP): "May He grant you out of the riches of His glory, to be strengthened and spiritually energized with power through His Spirit in your inner self, [indwelling you innermost being and personality], so that Christ may dwell in your hearts through your faith. And may you, having been [deeply] rooted and [securely] grounded in love, be fully capable of comprehending with all the saints (God's people) the width and length and height and depth of His love [fully experiencing that amazing, endless love]; and [that you may come] to know [practically, through personal experience] the love of Christ which far surpasses [mere] knowledge [without experience], that you may be filled up [throughout your being] to all the fullness of God [so that you may have the richest experience of God's presence in your lives, completely filled and flooded with God Himself]."

Take this word and take it to heart. We are healed when we turn to his Spirit and allow his deep love to permeate our body, soul, and spirit. This translates into a renewed perspective of our mind towards our bodies and how we treat them moving forward. Receiving this level of healing erases self-rejection and replaces it with a healthy perspective on how we are made.

What Are the Evidences of Self-Rejection?

Self-rejection shows up in many forms and often infiltrates through the mind. We believe lies about ourselves and our bodies that don't line up with what God says about us in Scripture. Recognize your need to accept God's design for your body in how he made you. Individuals who demonstrate the following traits may struggle with self-rejection:

- **Inability to Trust God**

    If a person rejects God's design for his physical appearance, he probably will have difficulty putting confidence in the Designer's plan for other areas of his life.

    . . . .

- **Self-Criticism**

    Complaints about unchangeable physical features, abilities, parentage, and social heritage are indications of self-rejection.

- **Wishful Comparison with Others**

    Desiring to be different in areas that cannot be changed is a clear evidence of self-rejection. *". . . Shall the thing formed say to him that formed it, why hast those made me thus?"* (Romans 9:20).

- **Floating Bitterness**

    Many people have said "I hate myself!" They may be referring to their words or actions in the past, or they may be referring to their whole being. In the latter case, their final hatred will be directed toward the One Who made them.

- **Perfectionism**

    It is healthy to want to do our best, but when the time expended outweighs the value of the accomplishment, it is an indication of self-rejection—condemning your best as "never good enough."

- **Attitudes of Superiority**

    A person with an attitude of superiority feels inferior but is trying to narrow his field of comparison.

- **Wrong Priorities**

    Self-rejection may be reflected in a neglect of God-given responsibilities in order to spend much time in pursuit of that which could bring acclaim from others.[2]

Dealing with self-rejection requires turning to God, thanking Him for how he made you, and understanding the reality of who you are in Christ. Meditate on the truth of Scripture and what God says about you. For example, Psalm 139:13–14 (NIV) says, "You knit me together in my mother's womb. I praise you because I am fearfully and wonderfully made." The God of the universe tells us we are each unique, worthy, and chosen. The list above shows what can happen when we do not believe our identity in Christ. By knowing what God says about us, we can step into the destiny he has for us through the Holy Spirit. Let the Holy Spirit show you where you need to change, and step forward into what he has created for you.

"Self-Rejection: Its Characteristics, Causes, and Cures"

Self-rejection, according to Dr. Charles Stanley in a radio message on the topic, is a form of bondage that causes us to project our negative feelings about ourselves on others. The biblical definition of self-rejection is a sinful response to our circumstances. Stanley bases this definition on Colossians 1:21–22 (NIV): "Once you were alienated from God and were enemies in your minds because of your evil behavior. But now he has reconciled you by Christ's physical body through death to present you holy in his sight, without blemish and free from accusation." People with self-rejection tendencies have chronic feelings of unworthiness and are willing to base their self-worth on opinions of others rather than on their relationship with God. Dominating the thoughts of a person feeling self-rejection is this: "I must please these people in my life in order to feel good about myself."

Feelings of self-rejection turn up in many situations and through multiple channels. Characteristics of people feeling self-rejection can include the following:

- Overemphasis on dress (a self-image problem)

- Difficult time trusting God- Difficult time loving others/being loved by others (psychic determinism/childhood hurts)
- Critical spirit- Feelings of inferiority/inadequacy
- Anger
- Perfectionism ("I must be perfect to feel good about myself; arrogance and pride feelings are really cover-ups for insecurity.")
- Easily hurt
- Suspicion of others [sic] actions
- Self-isolation (that way, the only one that rejects them is themselves)
- Depression (because you failed your expectations)
- Self-verification (of their worthiness/self-worth)
- Sensual fantasies (not a matter of sexual morality, it's a matter of acceptance)
- Domineering the circumstances[3]

The characteristics of people dealing with self-rejection point us toward the solution of Jesus. The goal is to work through self-rejection with the help of the Holy Spirit to get to a point where if someone rejects you, your self-worth is not based on that individual's opinion but on God's. According to Dr. Stanley, there are three feelings needed for one to be emotionally healthy: feelings of belonging, feelings of worthiness, and feelings of competence. Self-worth should be based upon what God says, which according to Stanley looks like this: "I have a sense of worth — Jesus died for me; I have a sense of competence — the Holy Spirit is working in me."[4]

There are multiple ways to break free from self-rejection and self-contempt. We must identify the feelings of rejection and then replace the root lie with God's truth. What does God's word say about your worth? Find those scriptures, and then thank the Father that you are unconditionally loved, completely forgiven, totally accepted, and complete in Christ. From there, you will come out from under the oppression of self-rejection and self-abuse and become the woman or man you are destined to be—a secure, confident, amazing, worthy child of God, who knows their God and is willing to stand firm in the faith of their Father. The Father beckons us to come, taste, and see his goodness now, in the land of the living. But first we must let go and place his truth about who we are in the innermost place.

Your Innermost Place

Where is your innermost being or place? It is your heart. God comes to enter your heart through salvation. He makes his dwelling inside each of us who have accepted him as Lord and Savior. What is amazing is the way he made each of us.

Your makeup has three parts: body, soul, and spirit. Your body is the vessel that houses your soul and spirit. Your soul is where God resides (i.e., inside your heart), and your spirit is your connection with the Holy Spirit. When God says he wants truth in your innermost place (Psalm 51:6 says, "Surely you desire truth in the inner parts; you teach me wisdom in the inmost place"), he means he wants you to replace all lies with the truth of who he says he is about you and who he wants you to be. Two lies I once believed were "I have to be skinny to be pretty" and "If I was taller, my weight wouldn't matter and I would be loved because tall people are more model-like." God graciously replaced those lies with the truth that I am "fearfully and wonderfully made." Walking away from the self-abuse of food cleanses, trying to hit a certain number on the scale, was a difficult challenge. The truth is, our bodies change over time due to hormones, having children, and our metabolism eventually slowing down. These facts do not negate the truth of who God made me to be, which is a daughter of the Most High, wonderfully and beautifully made.

It can take time to let this truth sink into our souls. But when we constantly fight against how he made us through self-rejection and self-abuse, we end up compromising our purpose and our makeup. There is a reason the Bible says to guard our hearts. Proverbs 4:23 (TPT) says, "So above all, guard the affections of your heart, for they affect all that you are. Pay attention to the welfare of your innermost being, for from there flows the wellspring of life." From the heart flows all the life gifts the Father wants to give us. Life gifts include abundance, joy, kindness, gentleness, patience, joy, and love. But if we do not love and protect our hearts from what the world says, we settle for earthly wisdom in our innermost being. The last thing God wants is for his truth to be quenched in our hearts. He wants our hearts to come fully alive in him and in his truth. He wants those life gifts to become fully present in our lives, making us different from the world. The Bible says we are to be in the world, but not of the world. We as believers are to look, think, and act differently than what is around us. This all starts in the innermost place.

Here are several ways to guard your innermost being:

1. Actively read and memorize his Word. Those truths become placed in our hearts through knowing his Word.
2. Actively sit, rest, and take time to pray. The ability to hustle is not a fruit of the spirit. We are to take the time to develop a relationship with the Father. Relationships take time and intention. How often are in you intentional with the Father?
3. Take ten minutes of silence each day. Start your quiet time with ten minutes of silence. This allows you to quiet your mind and then ask the Holy Spirit, "What is on your heart today? What word do you want me to study? How can we partner together today?"

4. Soak in the presence of God. How often do we finish our quiet time and rush off to begin or end our day? Abiding in the presence of the Father radically transforms us.
5. Take communion for a week. Write down your observations, thoughts from the Holy Spirit, and what scripture the Lord takes you through. This gift of salvation is to be celebrated, and it brings us into communion with him. He died for us! Let us celebrate this provision with reverence.

When we have truth in our innermost being, we know which way to go because of the scriptures placed deep within us. The heart, in biblical language, is the center of the human spirit, from which spring emotions, thoughts, motivations, courage, and action—i.e., "the wellspring of life" (Proverbs 4:23 TPT). The heart is explained multiple times through the Psalms and Proverbs. Our hearts are regenerated when filled with the Holy Spirit. Our hearts will get confused and make poor choices (i.e., sin, which is choosing anything other than God), but in the end, with the indwelling of God in our innermost place, our hearts become remade into something new that helps us to guard against the ways of the world. We are to guard against any wickedness taking root in our hearts and not quench the Spirit within us. In Mark 7:20–22 (NIV), Jesus tells us what comes from our hearts when wickedness takes root in our innermost being: "What comes out of a person is what defiles them. For it is from within, out of a person's heart, that evil thoughts come—sexual immortality, theft, murder, adultery, greed, malice, deceit, lewdness, envy, slander, arrogance, and folly. All these evils come from inside and defile a person." These things are what come out of our hearts if we are not consecrated to the Lord. God is there making our hearts and souls into his image. We are saved once and redeemed every day until we reach glory.

Truth in the Innermost Place

God desires to place his truth within the recesses of your heart. To fully walk in freedom and allow our innermost being to be filled with his truth, we must rightly position ourselves before the Father. So many things come at us that plant seeds of insecurity—e.g., the message that we must look a certain way to be loved—but we need to realize those things are other people's stuff. We cannot let their stuff, their unhealed trauma and hurts, affect us, nor can we take on others' thoughts and pain as our own.

One story comes to mind as I was walking out my freedom from self-abuse. We have generational sin around self-abuse and a physical manifestation of this in my family is hiatal hernias. As I walked through a significant healing session where we unearthed the issues of self-abuse in my house, I was radically healed in my stomach. When I went to the doctor for a scope due to some stomach issues, they mentioned there was no hiatal hernia. It was completely gone! One way self-abuse manifests itself is in the stomach causing GI issues. Our thought life is tied physically to so many parts of our bodies, especially our stomach and intestines. Imagine walking out your healing and it radically changing the scope of your inner being? This is what happens when we come out from under self-hatred and walk into freedom.

Our minds are tied to our hearts, and this is where we need to battle for right thinking As Romans 12:2 (NIV) tells us, "Do not conform to the pattern of this world, but be transformed by the renewing of your mind. Then you will be able to test and approve what God's will is—his good, pleasing and perfect will." Our overall health is tied to knowing what God says about who we are and whose we are. What God has for each person is uniquely given by him. We are to orient our minds to the mind of Christ; the outcome is to be who we are naturally. You are loved amazingly and perfectly right where you are. Do you know this?

Once our hearts and minds get rightly aligned with Christ, we begin to see how our wrong thinking keeps us in bondage to self-rejection and self-abuse. There are so many deceptions in the world, the desire for control being one of those deceptions. This circular pattern of bondage (control and self-rejection) by the enemy keeps us from getting free, happy, and completely integrated. The Holy Spirit and God can do things we cannot even fathom, and this means helping us become emotionally, physically, and spiritually integrated beings. Isn't this amazing?

By partnering with God, we can walk in fullness and have permission to walk in freedom. Through the anointing of the Spirit and walking in right relationship with Christ, we come into alignment and freedom. We have authority where we are free (meaning this issue of self-rejection and self-abuse no longer has any power or authority over us). Any sort of self-abuse destroys any spiritual authority that you carry. The enemy does not want you to succeed. By having the mind of Christ, proactively rehearsing what is positive and true, we partner with Christ in the truth of who we are in him and how to love ourselves rightly. Our outward projection ends up becoming a true reflection of our inward reality, and this ultimately will reflect the love of the Father. This freedom and truth in our innermost being allows him to fulfill all his plans for us. His good gifts are secure: "LORD, you alone are my portion and my cup; you make my lot secure" (Psalm 16:5 NIV). But if we do not partner with him, we will miss the good gifts he has for us because we are in bondage to the enemy. As we abide in Christ, place his truth in our innermost being, we lean into all his good gifts for our life. What an amazing opportunity to celebrate being in relationship with the Creator of the universe! He beckons each of us into relationship with him, and his good gifts are waiting to be received once we walk out from under self-abuse and self-rejection.

Kim Dolan Leto offers a powerful prayer to end our discussion here on finding freedom from self-contempt: "Dear God, Thank you for creating me with a unique look, shape, and size. Your Word says that I am fearfully and wonderfully made. Help me to walk in that godly confidence. Empower me in my insecurity to roll my shoulders back, pick my head up, and smile, knowing I am a one-of-a-kind, God-designed daughter of the King. Your Word says I am the work of your hand and that you see my heart, Lord. Let the beauty of this truth fill me up so I can see myself through your eyes. In Jesus's name, amen."[5]

Scripture around Freedom from Self-Contempt and Self-Abuse

- Romans 8:1 (NIV): "Therefore, there is now no condemnation for those who are in Christ Jesus."
- Psalms 51:6 (WEB): "Behold, you desire truth in the inward parts. You teach me wisdom in the inmost place."
- Psalm 16:5 (NLT): "Lord, you alone are my inheritance, my cup of blessing. You guard all that is mine."

- Philippians 1:6 (NIV): "being confident of this, that he who began a good work in you, will carry it on to completion until the day of Christ Jesus."

- Psalm 138:8 (ESV): "The LORD will fulfill his purpose for me; your steadfast love, O LORD, endures forever. Do not forsake the work of your hands."

- Colossians 1:21–23 (NIV): "Once you were alienated from God and were enemies in your minds because of your evil behavior. But now he has reconciled you by Christ's physical body through death to present you holy in his sight, without blemish and free from accusation—if you continue in your faith, established and firm, and do not move from the hope held out in the gospel. This is the gospel that you heard and that has been proclaimed to every creature under heaven, and of which I, Paul, have become a servant."

- Isaiah 46:3–4 (NKJV): "Listen to me, O house of Jacob, And all the remnant of the house of Israel, Who have been upheld by Me from birth, Who have been carried from the womb: Even to your old age, I am He, And even to gray hairs I will carry you! I have made, and I will bear; Even I will carry, and will deliver you."

Unleash the Box

1. Self-rejection and self-abuse is like a prison. Set the captives free! Where is self-abuse keeping you bound up?
2. God desires truth in your innermost place—the truth of who he is and how he sees you. What is holding you back from believing his truth about you? Who has God made you to be?
3. How can you let the waves of his love wash over you? Do you love yourself? Do you like who you are?
4. What are you rejecting in yourself?
5. What and who are you valuing more than yourself?
6. How will you let the Holy Spirit show you the worth you possess? He truly desires to show each of us kindness and goodness in our innermost beings.

7. Over time, the more our self-worth is based on the truths in God's Word, we will gain a better understanding of ourselves, God, and others. If our self-concept is off, we will not be able to perceive others the way they deserve to be understood. How might your self-worth be off?

Prayer: We pray for each person to have the courage to show up for this process. Give them renewed energy and strength as they watch every promise become fulfilled before their eyes. Help them to taste abundant life and to rest in their heart more than any other thing. We know your goodness, kindness, and faithfulness are tangible, and we count the ways we have tasted and seen them. Cover and surround each person with your nearness and presence. Go before them, creating paths of peace, and may they not know want. In Jesus's name, amen.

Chapter 4: Finding Freedom and Wholeness in Health

If I keep God in a box, he can't disappoint me. And if I keep God in a box, then I can believe him for things, and choose to say because he didn't answer that or he didn't deliver on that, he chooses not to. I knew he could but didn't know if he would.

—Tina Hansen

Tell yourself out loud, "You are no longer stuck. You are no longer powerless. You are seen. You are known. And you are deeply loved exactly as you are. Created perfectly by a God who does not make mistakes, Kelly, inner healer counselor."

Health is a tricky subject for most people. Either you are free from medical issues, or you are dealing with some curveball's life has thrown your way. My health has sent me in and out of different doctors' offices, all the while trying to find the right medical care plan.

When I finally came to the end of searching for the next cure, it occurred to me I was not taking this part of my life to Jesus. If Jesus came to heal the sick, why couldn't he heal me? He ended up healing me in a combination of ways through the help of a naturopath, medical doctor, and inner healing counselor. When we pay more attention to other voices in our lives (family, friends, counselors, our behaviors, doctors, etc.,) than to the Holy Spirit inside of us, it can create emotional, physical, and spiritual unhealth. This is what had happened in my life. I was not healthy from the inside out. My body was not cooperating because I had not dealt with the unhealthy reality of what was going on inside me—anger, control, and comparison—and how it was affecting everything and everyone in my circles. I took my unhealthy realities out on the people closest to me by being judgmental, critical, and unhappy.

What is amazing is that when the Lord chases you down and says, "Let us end this journey together well. I want to heal you," you pay attention. Taking the time to bring this area of your life under the lordship of his majesty will reap amazing dividends in your future. Healing of health issues is possible.

Finding Freedom during Health Issues

The year 2019 had brought yet another physical health challenge for me. From 2012 to 2017, my body and I had been on a health roller coaster through multiple life-changing surgeries, including thyroid cancer removal. As we walked through the prospect of another surgery in 2019, this time in my shoulder, I kept thinking of all the amazing gifts my family and I had been given. My family and I could walk, talk, see, and hear. Those were the things I needed to hold on to as I faced yet another surgery. Here is some practical advice I've collected over the seasons of contending for my healing in my health journey.

Put one foot in front of the other.

You get up each day and make the decision to keep moving forward. My mentor has a saying: "You keep on, keeping on." It does not mean you don't question or think of the what-ifs. You certainly can, but in addition, take each health hardship to the Lord to see what he wants to say and have you learn through it. He can deliver you from allowing the health hardship to affect your quality of life.

Face the health hardship straight-on.

One of my friends' fathers was diagnosed with cancer earlier this year. He is in the process of doing chemo and radiation every week. Even though we are across the country from one another, we talk weekly for support. This friend has also helped me face several of my own health crises head-on. Whatever sickness or affliction you are facing, collect all the info and make a game plan. There are multiple questions to ask when faced with these situations:

- What is the Lord saying about this situation?
- How is the Spirit leading you to pray? What scripture can we pray over the one who is ill and their situation (even if it's yourself)? If you are in the proximity of the person or need prayer yourself, lay hands on them or have someone lay hands on you. James 5:14 (AMP) says, "Is anyone among you sick? He must call for the elders (spiritual

leaders) of the church and they are to pray over him, anointing him with oil in the name of the Lord."

- What steps and treatment plans are there that will help?
- What support is needed? Is it meals, car rides, child care, etc.?

Taking it to the Lord, making a game plan, figuring out the costs, and moving forward can help anyone face these types of health hardships.

Find your joy and hold on.

Viewing life as a gift is so vital to resilience during a health crisis. What makes you feel joy, smile, or laugh? Find it and hold on tight. We all will face health issues as we age. We think we are never going to have aches and pains, but it happens. I have learned not to it let get me down, and in those moments my kids remind me how to laugh. They help me see how important laughter is when walking through health issues.

Coming out on the other side of thyroid cancer made me stronger, as I had to learn how to hold on to joy. My friend's father puts one foot in front of the other when he thinks he cannot. Health issues end up showing you that freedom is possible. It is within reach to cultivate freedom in our mentality, in putting one foot in front of the other, and in finding joy. So, "keep on keeping on"—each health issue you face can make you stronger.

Healing and Deliverance from Health Hardships

What if you surrendered your healing to the Lord? The Creator of the universe wants to heal you from all heartache and hardship and bring you into a joy that makes you giggle with endless abundance.

A friend's journey with liver issues really brought the healing journey into perspective for me. God used this time to draw me near and root my confidence in him so I would be prepared to walk through my own liver journey one year later.

God began giving my friend words from every direction that God would heal her. I knew he was asking me to believe for the healing, but I did not understand how he would heal her. A few months later she sensed the Holy Spirit saying the liver was a physical manifestation of an emotional and spiritual reality. Then she started praying for leading, and God eventually led her to someone who does inner healing prayer. During the first meeting, this woman read a list of the things God had shown her about my friend whom she'd never met. One thing the woman said was, "You are storing anger in your liver." It was uncanny how it lined up with other details she did not know, but I was shocked. My friend had done counseling, done her work, and she can tell you her story, but she believed she was free. What my friend learned was she was only cognitively free; she had understanding and had broken down the lies and behavioral patterns that had caused her pain in the past. But she had never released the emotions she needed to release at the time, ones she had been too unhealthy to feel. She had dealt with the surface but had not emptied her "container," her body, of the old unhealthy emotional realities weighing her down. It was amazing what the Holy Spirit, through prayer, highlighted that had not been dealt with, but God used all of it. This reminds us to increase our paradigm, never assuming that medical doctors always have the full picture!

My friend's journey above paints a true picture of what healing can look like when we step into faith and allow God to heal us from the inside out. This is how the Lord works in our lives—stripping away the old and replacing it with his truth.

Divine Healing

Reading the New Testament, we see a multitude of examples of healing. The New Testament teaches us, in 1 Corinthians 12 regarding spiritual gifts, to believe in the gift of healing among the many spiritual gifts that God bestows to his children and refuse to reinterpret it. God tells us to hold firmly to the Scriptures and at the same time pray to God to elevate our experiences. God doesn't want us to lower Scripture to the level of our experience. Our experience is to be elevated to Scripture. How do we do this? We can pray for those who need healing and trust that God will respond. John Wimber said, "I would rather pray for one hundred people to be healed and only see one healed and 99 go unhealed, then not to pray for anybody and all 100 go unhealed."[1] It is worth it to see one truly delivered from affliction. We should not let the absence of our experience or our healing cause us to disobey his Word. We believe for the healing even when we don't see it before our eyes. Below are twelve characteristics of Jesus's healing ministry while on earth, delineated by Dr. Sam Storms in his podcast exploring *Word and Spirit,* which give us a picture of what is possible when walking out our healing.

Twelve Characteristics of Jesus's Healing Ministry

1. Jesus healed hundreds if not thousands of people (Matthew 4:23–24 ESV: "healing every disease and every affliction").

2. No one Jesus touched was left unhealed. This tells us God's heart is to heal. God, the Father, and Holy Spirit have a tremendous heart and an affection for those who are hurting, and they love to see people set free from disease and sickness.

3. Jesus never inflicted anyone with a disease and never suggested sickness is a blessing from God because you've been obedient—or a curse because you've been disobedient. In Luke 4:39, in fact, he rebuked illness. Jesus did tell us to expect persecution, but he never said any such thing about disease or sickness.

4. Jesus portrayed healing not only as a sign the kingdom was coming but as an essential element in God's kingdom. When the kingdom is present, people are healed. According to Luke 9:2, Jesus sent out his followers to proclaim the kingdom of God and heal others. That is what the kingdom of God is: God's sovereign power over sickness and demons and guilt.

5. Jesus healed people by the power of the Spirit (Luke 4:14–21; Matthew 12).

6. Most often, the healings of Jesus were instantaneous (Mark 8:22–26). Some were partial and gradual. What difference does it make if healing comes now or later? All that matters is that it comes at all. Healing is healing regardless of the timing.

7. Jesus's healings were subject to two factors: the presence or absence of faith and the purpose of his heavenly Father. Jesus never asked anyone if they believed it was his will to heal them. He did ask them if he was able to heal them

(Matthew 9:28). The role of faith is a significant one in determining the purpose of his heavenly Father.

8. Jesus believed that many but not all sicknesses, diseases, and afflictions were the work of Satan. Today in our churches many believe it is God who afflicts people with disease, which is not true according to Scripture. Healing is always the work of God.

9. Jesus identified some sickness as unrelated to personal sin and other as related to sin. The blind man who was healed had not committed any particular sin. The paralyzed man was healed, but Jesus commanded him not to let any sin cause illness for him again (John 5).

10. Jesus regularly healed the sick by laying hands on them. In Luke 4:40, Jesus laid hands on every sick person present and healed them.

11. Jesus never prayed for the sick to be healed. He commanded the paralyzed to get up and walk; he commanded the ears of the deaf to be opened, etc. It doesn't mean it's wrong to pray for the sick, but on

occasion God may grant us the gift of faith so we can speak more authoritatively than we might otherwise do: "Be healed in the name of Jesus." It does not always happen, but sometimes we are commanded to pray this way anyway.

12. Jesus was motivated by compassion. Jesus loved his followers and felt compassion for them. He was moved by his compassion. Mark 9:22 shows a man appealing to his compassion and hoping his son might be delivered. In Luke 7:13–14, Jesus tells the dead boy's mother not to weep and tells the boy to arise. The heart of Jesus is for a broken, sorrowful people. For example, Matthew 14:14 (NIV) tells us, "When Jesus landed and saw a large crowd, he had compassion on them and healed their sick."

Apart from Faith: A Miraculous Healing Journey

Tina Hansen is a dear friend who wrote this excerpt below. Her miraculous account of healing is God's story. We had the opportunity to walk through this journey together and it was a privilege to walk alongside her during this time. Hope you are as blown away at God's goodness as we continue to be.

As a Christ follower, faith has been something I have claimed for years. After all, how can you be a Christian without having faith? Do I believe God incarnate came to earth to suffer and die as the only suitable sacrifice to reconcile a sinful people to the Father? Near the end of 2018, after an arduous seven-year dark-night-of-the-soul journey, I sat alone taking stock of my heart and found something startling.

Peering into the depths of my being, I found a soul that was broken, battered, and bruised. It was an empty, dry, and desolate vessel. For the previous seven years, I had devoted myself to providing care to someone in my family. I was assisting with my loved one's extended physical, mental, and emotional struggles, all while dealing with my own battle with multiple sclerosis. I was not allowing Papa God to replenish what I was giving away. In light of this reality, it is no surprise I was experiencing a dark night of the soul.

Until that fateful day in 2018, I didn't have the margin, or quite honestly the capacity, to look beyond my next step. I was surviving only because my eyes were fixed on my circumstances. Then I suddenly recognized I had shifted my perspective from heavenly realities to earthly ones. I was mired down in the darkness of this world, and I felt stuck.

Taking the Next Step

For the first time in years, I cried out to the Lord. Not the passing prayers for strength, comfort, and rest I often whispered without thinking, but a beseeching wail of searching for hope. Though I would have told you I still believed in the God of the breakthrough, facing the condition of my heart and life,

I began to absorb that I did not know what I believed anymore. And that recognition shook me to my core.

Over the next few weeks I began a tentative dialogue with the Lord. I was testing Him. Was he listening? Would he respond? Would it change anything? Then one day the Lord invited me on a journey of restoration. Although I was eager to have the condition of my heart altered, I didn't readily accept his invitation. I was afraid. As I explored the basis of that fear, I realized if I were being completely honest, the fear was a lack of faith. The faith I had proclaimed was nothing more than cautious optimism. Because believing for something meant I had to risk my already fragile heart. What if disappointment happened instead of hope? What if the desires of my heart never materialized? How about my vulnerable heart?

In processing these questions, I came to understand my greatest worry wasn't about me at all, but about the One who held all my possibilities. It was at this moment the real issue came to light: I had lost my faith. In a misguided attempt to protect my heart, I had minimized the size of my God. If I did not expect him to move on my behalf, I wouldn't be destroyed if he chose not to move. This painful revelation became the foundation for my pursuit of the truth.

Discovering God

My quest began with wanting to discover who God was and determine for myself his nature and characteristics. Who was he to me, for me and in me? I knew I would first have to understand and embrace the meaning of genuine faith. This truth can be found in Hebrews 11:1 (AMP): "Now faith is the assurance (title deed, confirmation) of things hoped for (divinely guaranteed), and the evidence of things not seen [the conviction of their reality—faith comprehends as fact what cannot be experienced by the physical senses]." When I reread this scripture in the Amplified translation, the Holy Spirit highlighted two things for me. First, the opposite of faith is not doubt, which I had always presumed; it's sight. When we can clearly see what lies ahead, faith is not necessary. Secondly, faith cannot be embraced without fully expecting the fulfillment of things for which we hope.

    I wish I could tell you these realizations were sufficient to restore what was lost. These truths allowed me to take my first, guarded steps toward wholeness. As I walked deeper into my grand adventure with the Lord, he slowly revealed himself to me in big and small ways. With every new discovery, my faith grew firmer and surer. I came to comprehend that without faith I could not embrace the life he desired to give me. Hebrews 11:6 (AMP) says, "But without faith it is impossible to [walk with God and] please Him, for whoever comes [near] to God must [necessarily] believe that God exists and that He rewards those who [earnestly and diligently] seek Him."

You can listen to my story on the Amazing Grace Talk podcast with specifics about how my healing journey evolved with Papa God (with distinct to things Papa God needed to work out in me). However, I believe with all my heart what he did for me, he will do for you if you will allow him.

Full Restoration

My pilgrimage with the Lord has brought full restoration to my once shattered heart. As my inner healing happened, Papa went beyond my wildest expectations and brought complete physical healing from my twenty-year battle with multiple sclerosis and a host of other conditions. I stand today healed, whole and delivered. While the inner and physical restoration is such a gift, the greatest gift I received was discovering the gift giver.

What do you need to believe for today? Do you have faith with a capital *F*, or are you protecting your heart because of fear like I did? Fear of what might not manifest in the ways you desire? Friends, let me encourage you to examine your heart honestly and reach out to your Papa God, asking him to redeem and restore any broken pieces. And ask with expectation he will respond, because he "is able to [carry out His purpose and] do superabundantly more than all that we dare ask or think [infinitely beyond our greatest prayers, hopes, or dreams], according to His power that is at work within us" (Ephesians 3:20 AMP).

Isn't God amazing? Watching and praying with Tina as she walked through her healing journey gave me the courage to face health hardships with a new perspective. Tina weaned herself off all medication, walks and runs without any assistance, and is a living testimony to God's goodness. Healing is possible today. God still saves, delivers, redeems, and heals. We are in a season of believing God for signs, wonders and miracles. Become desperate for God and see what he does in your life.

Scripture around Freedom in Health

- Isaiah 54:17 (CSB): "No weapon formed against you will succeed."

- Galatians 2:20 (AMP): "I have been crucified with Christ [that is, in Him I have shared His crucifixion]; it is no longer I who live, but Christ lives in me. The life I now live in the body I live by faith [by adhering to, relying on, and completely trusting] in the Son of God, who loved me and gave Himself up for me."

- John 8:36 (AMP): "So if the Son makes you free, then you are unquestionably free."

- Isaiah 53:4–5 (NIV): "Surely he took up our pain and bore our suffering, yet we considered him punished by God, stricken by him, and afflicted. But he was pierced for our transgressions, he was crushed for our iniquities; the punishment that brought us peace was on him, and by his wounds we are healed."

- Jeremiah 17:14 (NIV): "Heal me, Lord, and I will be healed; save me and I will be saved, for you are the one I praise."

- James 5:14–15 (NIV): "Is anyone among you sick? Let them call the elders of the church to pray over them and anoint them with oil in the name of the Lord. And the prayer offered in faith will make the sick person well; the Lord will raise them up. If they have sinned, they will be forgiven."

- Jeremiah 30:17 (NIV): "But I will restore you to health and heal your wounds,' declares the Lord."

- Proverbs 4:20–22 (NIV): "My son, pay attention to what I say; turn your ear to my words. Do not let them out of your sight, keep them within your heart; for they are life to those who find them and health to one's whole body."

Unleash the Box

1. Where are you storing unhealth in your body, causing physical manifestations of illness?
2. Do you feel you can surrender every area of your health to the Lord? Why or why not?
3. Where is your unbelief hindering the Lord from working in all things?
4. What do you need to believe for today about your health and healing journey?
5. The fitness and health industry in the Western world is a control-oriented framework, including diet plans such as paleo or keto. They keep us out of balance. God's way, instead, is always inside out, not outside in. Choosing health is to be in an emotional relationship with good. For example, do I eat even when I am not hungry? Food is to be nourishing and enjoyed. How have you engaged with the fitness and healthy industry in our culture?

Ask the Holy Spirit to get to any root issue in your life or spirit that is in the way of healthy living. What is the Holy Spirit revealing to you as you pray?

Prayer: Father, you see and know all, and nothing is hidden from you. You know the root of what is going on with our bodies, and you have power to provide full and complete healing and freedom. May we walk with you into all that is ours in Christ. We ask you to guide each of us in the steps you would have us take, lead us into all truth and into your wisdom, and bring about your desired purposes in our lives every step of the way. Thank you for our ability to trust and rest in you! We know all things serve your great and mighty plan, and you cannot fail in the good plans you have for us. You are greater than any other thing; may we fully rest in you. In Jesus's name, amen.

Chapter 5: Finding Freedom and Wholeness in Relationships

Allowing Him to be God, not putting Him in a box, has given me back the "Firm Foundation" that He intends for all of us to stand on.

—Sherry Bradshaw

Relationships of all kinds and how they have evolved in my life have been a part of my "back side of the mountain" season. From pruning certain relationships, to facing my fears of what my relationships would look like moving forward, to ending and beginning new ones, the relational ups and downs in my life have been immense. So immense, I personally wrote about them for over a straight year on my blog. It was not only my own relationships but my children's relationships with their friends as well. How do we find freedom and wholeness in this area? We walk it out in our everyday lives, take each lesson and sift it through Scripture, bring it to the Lord in prayer, and seek deliverance from the Holy Spirit.

So where do we start? We start in knowing our identity in Christ and then recognize what needs to shift and change in our relationships. As we change, our circles change. Let us discuss how to navigate and flourish in this sea of change. As Henry Cloud says, "If some relationships don't end, your life cannot flourish."[1]

Rethinking Our Relationships

Nobody ever does anything great by themselves. Margaret Mead once said, "Never underestimate the power of a few committed people to change the world. Indeed, it is the only thing that ever has." Nothing of significance has ever been produced by an individual acting alone or in isolation: no products, no movies, no inventions. Not even the creation of the heavens and the earth. Tom Rath writes in his excellent book *Vital Friendships*, "Remove relationships from the equation and everything disappears."[2]

Relationships Shape You

Relationships are powerful because God uses them to shape the kinds of people we become. We largely become like the people we are closest to. Jim Rohn has said, "You are the average of the five people you spend the most time with." Our thoughts, feelings, and actions reflect our most intimate friendships. People rub off on us whether we realize it or not. This truth works for the positive and the negative. In Proverbs 13:20 (ESV), it is written, "Whoever walks with the wise becomes wise, but the companion of fools will suffer harm." The wisdom of the wise rubs off, while foolishness spreads the same way. We influence each other in deep, soul-forming ways, says Danny Anderson, pastor of Emmanuel Church in Central Indiana.

How Is This Principle Affecting You?

Is this truth helping you or harming you? Are the people around you helping you become a better person? A better employee? A better spouse? A better parent? Or are they dragging you down, causing you to drift from the person you long to be and know you should be? To leverage this principle for the positive, you must take two actions:

1. **You must be intentional.**

    We must choose our friends carefully. Our tendency is to choose friends quickly, based on superficial reasons. This is an area, though, where we must be extremely picky. We must set a standard for what kind of people we will allow close to us—close to what I call our "core."

    Think about your best friends right now. Can you honestly say they are the best influence on you? Do they encourage your faith? Do they take their relationships with God seriously? Do they intend to honor God with their lives? King David wrote, "I am a friend to anyone who fears you—anyone who obeys your commandments." (Psalm 119:63 NIV). Do you have at least two or three best friends who fear and obey God?

2. **You must prune your relationships.**

    Like every healthy rose bush that produces beautiful roses, your friendships need to be pruned. Henry Cloud uses this illustration in his book *Necessary Endings* to explain why if some relationships don't end, your life cannot flourish: "Without the ability to end things, people stay stuck, never becoming who they were meant to be, never accomplishing all that their talents and abilities should afford them."[3] Sometimes you can be a catalyst to change the focus and direction of a relationship. We can take the lead and say, "Jesus is going to be the focus of our relationship. We will seek to honor him in all things."

However, if we do not see a shift and the relationship continues to draw us away from Christ, we must end it. That is not to say we must remove the person from our lives. But it does mean it is time to push that person out of our "core"—to remove them from our sphere of influence.

You might be thinking, "If I follow this advice, I might not have any friends left!" Maybe. But is that so bad? You are bound to find new, better ones. And you always have God. He is always with you. He has promised never to leave you. And always remember this: having only a few friends, or even no friends, is better than having the wrong friends. The wrong friends will shape your life in the wrong way and take your life in the wrong direction.

Relationships: Rebuild or Walk Away?

The older you get, the harder it is to maintain friendships. Life ebbs and flows, friends move away, and people move on to other circles. Sometimes even additional health issues can cause people to walk away. During my cancer journey, a good friend of mine stopped being friendly. As we met to talk through our issues, it became clear this person had chosen to walk away during this time. They mentioned I had a negative health outlook that was brought on by my cancer and other health issues. Our conflict probably could have been resolved had I known sooner how this person was feeling about me.

Figure out if it is worth working through.

This conflict with my friend made me wonder, what do we do when someone we like, or love walks away? What would you do? This is a hard one to process. Ultimately, we need to take time to make sure both people in the relationship want to remain friends. Working through boundaries in regard to certain topics can help move the relationship forward. My friend and I had to do the hard work of figuring out what we could and could not talk about so that we could continue the friendship. That is never an easy conversation to have, but it's a necessary one. Some would think, "Well, is this truly a friend if I have to talk about these things with them?" The answer can be yes, and it depends on the situation and person. These types of conversations need to happen to ensure we're maintaining healthy relationships.

Examine whether they reciprocate your attention.

This keeps coming up for me personally. If someone will not hang out with you, text you back, or call you, then stop bothering with them. Time is so precious to everyone. You cannot get time back, so why waste it pursuing people who do not want to spend it with you? Find the people who love you for you and move on.

Find out why they walked away (if you can).

Sometimes it is best to let people walk away. There is a reason why they have left the friendship, and that is okay. If they are willing to talk, ask them what happened or what you may have done, if anything, to cause the conflict. They may say something as little as "You hurt me when you said this," or maybe they need space to figure out their own life situation.

Decide whether it is worth your time.

This is up to you and your friend. As friends we should clap loudest when someone we care about has good news. Your circle or core group of friends should want you to win in all aspects of life. If they do not, it's time to get a new circle. Our loudest cheerleaders need to be the circle of friends in our lives. One of my life themes this past year has been how to be a better friend who loves well. There are many components to that statement, but God has made it abundantly clear who to keep in my life and how to love those people well.

While it can be a very lonely season, there is always a reason behind these rebuilding times. God wants you to surround yourself with those who lift you up, help you flourish, and move you forward.

Sometimes this means stepping away and letting go. Other times it means figuring out how to make it work. Whatever friendship season you are in, know that God always wants what is best for you and your friends.

Rejection

So, what do you do when rejection occurs regardless of the efforts mentioned above? Rejection from others is awfully hard. My mom often says, "Man's rejection is God's protection." While true, this saying doesn't make it an easier road to walk. Sometimes our growth comes in the form of rejection. I personally went through a season of rejection that provided a ton of feedback on my life and allowed God to push me into a new realm of friendship with him. It helped me recognize where I needed to cut back on activities, who and where to invest my time, and how to help those who really need and want it.

Putting the Pieces Together

I had not put the pieces together of being in a rejection season until the Lord revealed it to me. During a Bible Study Fellowship meeting, it became very evident that I had been dealing with rejection in multiple areas and I needed to move forward and heal. This was shocking to me, but also very freeing. It helped to discover a label for what was going on.

Rejection can be extremely painful because it usually makes people feel as if they are not wanted, valued, or accepted. And unfortunately for me, I took the rejection from others as meaning I was not accepted or valued. How sad is it that we often react this way to other people's actions and their baggage? By not sticking to my boundaries, I let others' nonacceptance affect me significantly.

It is important to speak about it because we have a Savior who faced the ultimate rejection, and we should look to him as an example of how to respond. John 1:11 (NLT) tells us, "He came to his own people, and even they rejected him." Society may reject people based on religion, appearances, values, personality, or any number of other things. One way to overcome this in our own lives is to ask God,

"What is the purpose behind this season of rejection, and how can it help me become more Christlike?" So much easier said than done.

Here are some strategies to help you not take rejection personally:

- Remind yourself how much you are loved. There are several people who do love you: Father God, your family, your kiddos, etc. These are the people you need to surround yourself with every day.
- Remember, it is not always about you. Sometimes people are having a bad day, and their reaction has nothing to do with what you may have just said or done.
- Make sure you have good boundaries in place. Boundaries are essential to guarding your uniqueness as a person. (You can read more about boundary development at https://heathervshore.com/abuse-boundary-setting/).
- Make sure you have a support system, especially if you are sensitive to rejection. I did not realize I had this issue until it came up. My support system of family and friends helped

me work and think through how to protect myself and prioritize those most important to me.

- Reach out to those around you who are hurting. By focusing on others, you get your focus off yourself and onto those in need. This is something we all must prioritize; otherwise, it will not get done. It helps to focus on others' needs and stop worrying about what others think. Other people's problems are often much bigger than our own.

Always remember, replanting your tree a little further away from toxic people can help you grow. Rejection comes in many forms, and we should allow God to prune the toxic people from our lives. Rejection can also cause us to look forward to the good change coming while helping put all of our struggle into perspective. If you are going through rejection, whatever form, know you are loved and worth standing up for. There is a God who loves you and longs to make you free in this area. Allow him to show you your support system, people who can help you move on and turn this worldly reality into something otherworldly.

Friendship Lessons God Taught Me Through Children

Every time we go to the park, my son Harrison and daughter Maddie meet a new "friend." A couple of little boys and girls we've met have enjoyed playing with both my kids. They are fun kids to hang out with at the park. It's definitely fun to watch, but sometimes it's heartbreaking because they think everyone is their friend, even when they're not or when we'll never see them again.

These interactions have made me think about the friendship circles I have had in recent years. Going through a divorce and moving to different cities has led me to be a part of different groups through these different life seasons. Transitioning from married groups to single groups, back to married groups, and now groups with children has brought me full circle. Below is some friendship wisdom I've learned and hope to impart to my own children as they navigate making friends themselves.

Be yourself and you will find your people.

This is a difficult lesson for kids to learn. Do you remember those years when you wanted to please others to make friends? That is what playground experiences are all about, learning how to navigate friendships and be yourself. I want my kids to be loved for their exuberant personalities and joy for life. I want them to be liked for who they are. I'm trusting that teaching my kids to be themselves will help build their confidence in how God made them and lead them to finding their people.

Sometimes you will be friends for a season.

You will have friends who come and go based on where you are in life. This lesson has been particularly hard for me with friends moving on to other things in life. Sometimes these friends have been hard to let go of, and I must remember, those friends who are worth having will make the effort to reciprocate. I can only hope my kids learn this lesson more effortlessly than I have.

You do not have to be friends with everyone.

Social media will tell you differently, but you do not have to be friends with everyone. There is the assumption that quantity of friends means more than quality. There are circles of friends in life—your acquaintances, your friends who know you well, and then the two to three best friends who truly know you to the core. Those are the friends who have either walked life with you or whom God has knit together with you for a special purpose. I once attended a women's conference where a speaker said God had twelve friends and only two were his best friends. My hope is that my children will find the two or three friends who love them for who they are and are willing to stick by them through the good and the bad.

You are the company you keep.

There is a true adage that you are the company you keep. Putting boundaries in place to make sure you are friends with people who share the same values is especially important. Having gone through the process of boundary setting in my own life, I hope to impart this type of wisdom to my kids. You will have friends, but you want friends who value the same things as you and who treat you with the respect you deserve. My wish is to impart this wisdom to my children before they reach the teenage years when the company their keep will make or break their futures. God has shown me that these lessons will help our kids navigate making lifelong friends who love them as much as we do.

The Importance of Gathering

After God showed me these various lessons, I realized it was time to start gathering with others more. Life is not meant to be spent alone. To gather is bringing together people with common interests or getting people together for a movement. The people I know and gather with are from different areas of life where we have common interests. They can be from work, church, the gym, or the neighborhood. It is the common connection with these people that leads to gathering. In Christian circles people often call it "doing life together."

Doing life together is the Christian marketing term for community. God designed each of us to live in community and to grow in our walk with Christ. Part of the way this happens is to make sure you are not doing life alone. God provides freedom to gather when we realize we do not have to be perfect to gather with others. Whether it is through a church or some other avenue, you realize when you gather that people are flawed yet long for connection. We do not have to be independent from others. We, as people, are designed for community. Community is also what is often missing from our society. Unless awful natural disasters like Hurricane Harvey happen, we tend to do life only interested in ourselves. Whether it is during the hard times or good times, we should help carry each other's burdens and joys.

We must learn to create a safe place where people can share what is going on in their lives. This builds trust and helps bridge the gap to something greater, where we learn to depend on one another. This requires us being open to others and sharing things we may not want to share so others can bear our burdens and provide for our needs. It also requires a trust and an ability to cry with others or simply to listen. When others take the leap and talk openly, we need to receive them and have a passion for their lives so that the pool they jump into is not found empty and unwelcoming.

God gathered and cared for the feeblest and weakest of his people. Stepping out of your comfort zone and taking care of those around you can be tiring but also the most rewarding work. Isaiah 40:11 (NIV) sums it up well: "He tends his flock like a shepherd. He gathers the lambs in his arms and carries them close to his heart; he gently leads those that have young."

Sometimes God has us unlearn certain things and brings about tough and honest questions to ask ourselves: "Am I seeking community, and are there people in my life I trust? Who can I trust with my inner life, and who gets to speak truth into my situation? How can I walk more closely with Jesus and others? Am I attempting to do life on my own? How can I love others well?" These hard questions challenged me after being on the back side of the mountain and the pruning of friendships took place. God helped moved me past all of this to find healing, comfort, and even a new community group. My hope for this season in life is to build relationships and to love others well.

Find Those Who Lift You Up

I recently heard the *School of Greatness* podcast with Bob Goff. Bob Goff is a brilliant author, lawyer, humanitarian, and Christian. He said, "There's room for about eight people around your bed when you die. What if you figure out who your eight people are?"[4]

Never thought about it this way. As you grow and change, your eight will change! Who you start your life with will be different than who you end your life with at your bedside. God encourages us in our friendships, often using our friends to work in our lives. He provided David comfort through Jonathan and the loyalty of others. This gave David reassurance and intimacy with the Lord, which is recorded in God's Word to strengthen his people. Will you ask God to teach you how your union with him fills you and overflows to all your other relationships? He will show you how to make all your relationships whole and free.

Scripture around Freedom in Relationships

- Proverbs 13:20 (NKJV): "He who walks with wise men will be wise, but the companion of fools will be destroyed."
- 1 Corinthians 15:33 (NIV): "Do not be misled: 'Bad company corrupts good character."
- Proverbs 27:10 (NLT): "Never abandon a friend — either yours or your father's. When disaster strikes, you won't have to

ask your brother for assistance. It's better to go to a neighbor than to a brother who lives far away."

- Proverbs 12:26 (NIV): "The righteous choose their friends carefully."

- John 15: 12–13 (NIV): "My command is this: Love each other as I have loved you. Greater love has no one than this: to lay down one's life for one's friends."

Unleash the Box

1. Am I building a friendship with God? When you build friendship first with God and on the foundation of his Word, friendship gets fun. If you need hope in friendship, ask him!
2. Whom do you need to spend more time with?
3. What relationships in your life might need to be pruned?
4. What toxic people need to be removed from my life?
5. Am I seeking community? Are there people in my life I trust?
6. Who has access to me, and who has the guts to speak truth into my life?

7. Only God can fill the hole in our hearts. Friends are an added bonus. Who in my life could become a new friend?
8. Am I attempting to do life on my own? How can I love others well?

Prayer: Papa God, thank you for the relationships in my life. Help me to be a better friend to those around me. Fill up the hole in my heart first, so we can flow over into others' lives. Guide us as we walk in relationship with you and others. Let your love overflow. In Jesus's name, amen.

Chapter 6: Finding Freedom and Wholeness in Financial Decisions

*The lions may grow weak and hungry, but those who seek the L*ORD *will lack no good thing. Thank You for the great promise that I shall lack no good thing.*

—Psalm91.com

This is painful to write, but two years ago I was scammed out of thousands of dollars. It caused severe financial stress in our marriage and on our finances. Ironically, it also set us on a path toward financial freedom. We both wanted to get there but were lacking the discipline at the time to make this possible. God soon got ahold of our hearts and started to set us straight. He impressed upon us that he wanted the first fruits of what he had given us. As Malachi 3:10 (NIV) says, "'Bring the whole tithe into the storehouse, that there may be food in my house. Test me in this,' says the LORD Almighty, 'and see if I will not throw open the floodgates of heaven and pour out so much blessing that you will not have room enough to store it.'" Now, if you are like me and holding onto old paradigms, this sounds a lot like the prosperity gospel preached in some American churches. God is not saying, "I am a genie and will give you whatever you pray for in my name." He says, "Test me in this and see how I respond to your faithful obedience to give back a tenth of what I have already given you."

    This revelation was buried deep down in my innermost being, as I heard God saying, "I will provide for you." My natural response was still from a poverty mind-set, and God needed to set me free from this mind-set. How that looks in our natural, everyday lives may not be how we think it should look. However, we are to trust the Father and see that he is good. The Bible says, "Seek first his kingdom and his righteousness, and all these things will be given to you as well" (Matthew 6:33 NIV). God continually kept bringing this verse to my attention through my prophetic friends, through random prophets at Subway, and in literal signs that now hang on the wall in my house.

The problem was I was walking through a season where I was allowing the circumstances of my life to dictate my response to the trials I was facing. One of the trials involved my marriage, where I worried, "How will you provide for me if my marriage fails?" I kept thinking, "I am not good at marriage, and now my second marriage has not worked out. How will you work this out, Lord?" Our sweet Jesus reminded me, in him all things are possible. There is no striving for those connected to the vine of life, and he who began a good work in me would see it through to the end—such amazing promises that allow us to live above our circumstances and not be swayed by the emotions of life. This is where financial freedom is possible. When we stay connected to the vine, we learn not to let emotions sway our thoughts about our checkbooks or savings accounts. So where do we start with our finances?

Start with the Basics

I grew up in a paradigm of working for the same company until you retired. Retirement isn't even biblical, but that is another conversation for another time. You went to college, graduated, and then worked at the same company until it was time to hang up your hat. This never sat well with me. Why on earth would you not want to grow your life into something bigger, God-ordained, or, dare I say, a dream?

God places dreams in our hearts. Sometimes they are big dreams; sometimes they are small dreams that only matter to us. For example, I always wanted to create a home of solace, heart, and community. It's a small dream with big implications depending on who comes through our door. We get our identity from what we are created to do. What are you created to do? It is partly how we define ourselves. This comes back into how we orient our life around career and financial provision.

What dreams are you chasing—yours or God's? It's okay to have dreams and desires, and he will give them to us if we delight in him first (Psalm 37:4). Have you sat down with God and dreamed about and imagined where he wants to use you, your gifts, and your talents? He has uniquely gifted you to stand in our identity and giftings and use them for his kingdom. Imagination is the place of conception and also the womb of faith, and the seed of this place is the Word of

God. Use your imagination hand-in-hand with the Word of God. He will show you what you are meant to be doing and in turn will lead you into provision as you step in accordance with him.

One note to consider is we can have a poverty spirit when it comes to imagination. are different types of poverty spirit, such as in imagination, courage, and self-perception. A poverty spirit keeps you from being all you are called to be, accepting limitations you were meant to accept. Ask the Lord to show you where you are not believing God for his promises when it comes to provision.

Cultivate a Generous Heart/Spirit

Many Christians reduce their faith to a comfortable set of beliefs about God rather than an adventurous journey where he takes us beyond where we have been. This includes our hearts toward our finances and toward the provision he brings for his kingdom purposes. When we partner with God in what he wants to do, he sets in motion the ability for us to help and bless others.

Luke 6:38 (NKJV) tells us, "Give, and it will be given to you: good measure, pressed down, shaken together, and running over will be put into your bosom. For with the same measure that you use, it will be measured back to you." "Good measure" refers to the sufficiency of God and the fact that he is more than enough. When we see our cup overflowing, we may think it's waste. But God sees it as abundance. God wants what is in us to spill out of us, out onto the world around us, so that we're a blessing everywhere we go. The verse also says, "For with the same measure that you use, it will be measured back to you." If you use a spoon, it will be measured back to you with a spoon. If you use a giant bucket, it will be measured back to you with a giant bucket. Do you get it? This isn't about us living rich. But it is about us living prosperously and generously. When we give, God deposits back into our life, beyond what we could even dream.[1]

We Reap What We Sow

When I fell prey to being scammed by a fake missionary job, I was not trusting the Lord for provision. I could not get my eyes off my circumstances and how my life was falling apart before my eyes. I was only trusting myself and desperately needed a job, as I was going to be a single mom. How would I provide? How could I possibly find a job after six years of not working? Where did my hope come from?

The Lord gently reminded me of Matthew 6:33 and my need to re-evaluate how I looked at pain and consequences. How we look at pain is so important! Pain is the absence of pleasure, loss of control, heartache, not our choosing, discomfort, out of God's will, any situation that creates failed resources, loss of strength, fear, failure, hurt, and unmet expectations. If you look at the book of Job, you will find many explanations of pain. Ultimately, God is sovereign, Satan is God's tool, and God is completely in control.

How and where does pain come to us? It often comes mysteriously, as Job's example illustrates. Job was one of the holiest men in the Bible, and God allowed Satan to sift him (Job 1). Pain can come in the form of financial repercussions, illness, accidents, calamities, and unexplained tragedy. It can also come through cause and effect, as Galatians 6:7–8 (AMP) points out: "Do not be deceived, God is not mocked [He will not allow Himself to be ridiculed, nor treated with contempt nor allow His precepts to be scornfully set aside]; for whatever a man sows, this and this only is what he will reap. For the one who sows to his flesh [his sinful capacity, his worldliness, his disgraceful impulses] will reap from the flesh ruin and destruction, but the one who sows to the Spirit will from the Spirit reap eternal life." We reap what we sow, not only for ourselves but for others, in our own choices and sin habits. We are to take responsibility only for our own sin, not someone else's.

We will have trials from living a godly life. As 1 Peter 4:12 (AMP) reminds us, "Beloved, do not be surprised at the fiery ordeal which is taking place to test you [that is, to test the quality of your faith], as though something strange or unusual were happening to you." Likewise, 2 Timothy 3:12 (AMP) says, "Indeed, all who delight in pursuing righteousness and are determined to live godly lives in Christ Jesus will be hunted and persecuted [because of their faith]." At times, like the example of being scammed out of money, we also receive discipline from the hand of God. Hebrews 12:7–11 (AMP) makes this clear:

> You must submit to [correction for the purpose of] discipline; God is dealing with you as with sons; for

what son is there whom his father does not discipline? Now if you are exempt from correction and without discipline, in which all [of God's children] share, then you are illegitimate children and not sons [at all]. Moreover, we have had earthly fathers who disciplined us, and we submitted and respected them [for training us]; shall we not much more willingly submit to the Father of spirits, and live [by learning from His discipline]? For our earthly fathers disciplined us for only a short time as seemed best to them; but He disciplines us for our good, so that we may share His holiness. For the time being no discipline brings joy, but seems sad and painful; yet to those who have been trained by it, afterwards it yields the peaceful fruit of righteousness [right standing with God and a lifestyle and attitude that seeks conformity to God's will and purpose].

When pain comes into our lives, it behooves all of us to go before the Lord with our questions. The trials that come will point us to the one who knows all and can answer our questions.

Pain Exposes Different Life Lessons

Pain may display sin because of the choices we make, which is choosing something other than God. Pain can reveal a lack of character development where hope, patience, and discipline need to be developed. It can also show us what lies we are believing about God and where we are off in our self-perception. But one of the biggest life lessons pain shows us is where our trust is placed. Who are we really trusting? Is it us, our circumstances, or God? How can we come to him and ask him to rightly align our values to be in line with his will? Pain will not immediately go away, but in the surrender and trusting him to rearrange our lives to his values, we can expect things to shift and move. Only through surrendering to the Father can we build trust and grow our faith through our painful experiences.

Obedience and Dependence

When we align ourselves to his truth, believing in his promises, we do not need to plead for blessings; instead, we can just thank him for the blessings that will be inevitable. Blessings can be anything—a smile from a neighbor, a sunny day, or just sitting with him in his presence. Obedience to God without dependence on God is a burden, but when we unite obedience with dependence, his activity becomes the source of our activity. As Psalm 91:1–2 (NIV) says, "Whoever dwells in the shelter of the Most High will rest in the shadow of the Almighty. I will say of the LORD, "He is my refuge and my fortress, my God, in whom I trust." When his activity becomes our next step of obedience, we step into dependence on him. What step of obedience is he asking you to take that will require fully depending on him?

Test God and See

As the Lord kept speaking Matthew 6:33 over my life, he kept asking me to step into a new season where he would fulfill whatever was pruned from my life. Everything which God prunes, you can expect him to fulfill. He may not replace it right away with another natural provision, but he can and will be your more-than-enough in ways that will blow your mind and draw you deeper into his supernational power. He will be in every single thing he asks you to release in order to step into what he is purposing in your life. His intention is not for you to suffer, but for you to know first him and then his fulfillment in each area he is removing for a time. As referenced in chapter 5, for example, several friendships were pruned from my life because they weren't healthy for me. As a result of laying down what I thought friendship should look like, God started to reshape my idea of friendship and relationship. He has generously started placing healthier people into my life whose lives are aligned with the kingdom. When you steep your life in God's initiatives and provisions, you don't have to worry about missing out. You will find all your everyday human concerns will be met.

Scripture around Freedom in Finances

- Malachi 3:10 (NIV): "'Bring the whole tithe into the storehouse, that there may be food in my house. Test me in this,' says the LORD Almighty, 'and see if I will not throw open the floodgates of heaven and pour out so much blessing that you will not have room enough to store it.'"

- Matthew 6:33 (AMP): "But first and most importantly seek (aim at, strive after) His kingdom and His righteousness [His way of doing and being right—the attitude and character of God], and all these things will be given to you also."

- Matthew 6:33 (ERV): "What you should want most is God's kingdom and doing what he wants you to do. Then he will give you all these other things you need."

- Matthew 6:33 (GNT): "Instead, be concerned above everything else with the Kingdom of God and with what he requires of you, and he will provide you with all these other things."

- Isaiah 45: 6–7 (NLT): "So all the world from east to west will know there is no other God. I am the LORD, and there is no other. I create the light and make the darkness. I send good times and bad times. I, the LORD, am the one who does these things."

- Psalm 62:11–12 (NLT): "God has spoken plainly, and I have heard it many times: Power, O God, belongs to you; unfailing love, O LORD, is yours. Surely you repay all people according to what they have done."
- Psalm 119:68 (NIV): "You are good, and what you do is good; teach me your decrees."

Unleash the Box

1. Are you believing God for your provision in all things in your life? This includes physical, emotional, spiritual, and financial provision. What areas are you taking control for yourself?
2. Have you kept your eyes on circumstances and not on your God? What circumstances are you looking to yourself instead of God?
3. Are you seeking God's kingdom above all else? What obstacles are getting in the way?

4. What dream or dreams is God giving you to chase after? How does that line up with provision?

5. How is God asking you to walk in obedience when it comes to financial assets and gifts?

6. Where are you allowing a poverty spirit to infiltrate your imagination, courage, and expectations the Lord has for your life?

Prayer: Heavenly Father, thank you for the reminder that obedience to you must never be separated from dependence on you. May I experience a deeper realization of the ways you are working in and through me. May I release every provision burden I carry at your feet. Thank you for working on our behalf each and every day. In Jesus's name, amen.

Chapter 7: Finding Freedom and Wholeness in Parenting

If kids see parents whose significance is in Jesus, whose souls are satisfied in Jesus and they see the fruit of freedom in our own lives, that has a profound impact on them.

—Jeannie Cunnion

Parenting is a beautiful and wonderful journey. It is also some of the hardest work I've ever done. One of the things I struggled with early on was learning how to enjoy my little ones. There was so much pressure to do all these things, such as working a part-time job and taking care of a whole house with no help, that I missed out on enjoying every moment with them. While I can't go back, one thing the Lord showed me along the way was that our kids want relationship with us (just like God the Father wants relationship with us).

Relationship is more important than anything else. Kids want to know they are safe, loved, called, capable, and responsible. They want to know that no matter what they are loved. When we speak that truth into their lives, we allow them and ourselves as parents to walk toward freedom in parenting.

Letting Go of Other People's Opinions

One thing that was hard to navigate as a young mom was mom groups. Mom groups are filled with imperfect people trying to raise imperfect children. It is also filled with people who are grasping at straws to fill their lives with meaningless and trivial things. One of the fun lessons I learned from these groups was to let go of what others think. A lot of parents care about what others think, and I was one of those parents. I loved to ruminate on what others said and let it affect my actions. I came to realize I shouldn't care about other parents' opinions of me, but I should care about Jesus's opinion of me. His opinion matters most. It is human nature to want to be liked, but sometimes wanting to be liked comes at a cost when we aren't living out our purpose.

Another big lesson I learned early on in parenting was letting go of those who were not for me in the parenting journey. I started by developing a sense of self-worth through regular prayer. When we pray over ourselves with the truth of God, we start to believe the worth he has placed in each of us. We are all worthy and deserve to be treated with respect, especially by our kids. Part of letting go is figuring out who can speak into your life. Surround yourself with people who lift you up, do not gossip about you behind your back, and lean into God's truth.

God created all of us in his image. God's design is purposeful and perfect, and he created each one of us with unique gifts. Understanding what he says about you as a parent and your children will help lead you away from caring about others' opinions. One of my favorite verses is Ephesians 2:10 (NKJV): "For we are His workmanship, created in Christ Jesus for good works, which God prepared beforehand that we should walk in them." He says we are fearfully and wonderfully made, his workmanship, loved, and called into good works. When we take to heart others' opinions instead of what Jesus says, we set ourselves and our kids up to not follow our purpose.

Let God whisper into your heart the truth of who you are and whose you are. Filter the opinions of others through the reality that just because they think a certain way does not make it true. Be brave enough to accept negative feedback as a possible call to action, but not a definition of your identity. And while you may enjoy any positive feedback you receive, refuse to get bloated by it. We need to place our identifies in the unshifting grace of God, keeping our hearts attuned to the reassuring whispers of Jesus.[1]

If you or your child is called to something bigger than yourselves, do you let others' thoughts influence your decisions? This is where you can learn to let go, and here's why. Sometimes God will ask you to do something beyond your ability. This is amazing news! It should scare you, make you a little uneasy, because it's going to be big. So, ask God, "Can I trust you as we walk into this next endeavor?" Are you willing to say, "I will follow you, Jesus, wherever you lead"? If so, congratulate yourself because it is a great work only he can do. Believe in his leading and walk forward regardless of others. What is God calling you to do regarding this aspect of parenting?

Finding the Best Way to Raise Your Kids

All people regardless of age are created uniquely. We all show up on earth with a unique design and a unique call on our lives. This includes your children. As you learn your child's personality, temperament, likes and dislikes, interests, and all the other amazing things he or she is made of, you come to understand each child can require a different way to be raised. There are so many ways to raise your kids in truth and discipline. There's love and logic, discipline through connection, child-centered raising, and the list goes on and on. What is interesting is no one formula fits every kid because kids are all unique. This is where you must glean from experts, others who've gone before you, but also where you need to go to God and ask him, "What do I do in this moment? How do I raise this precious child you've given me?" This is why it's vital to let go of others opinions because no one size fits all in the realm of parenting. What worked for your parents may not work for you.

I had to let go of control to let my kids help me clean the house—i.e., I had to realize it doesn't have to be cleaned my way. They needed to learn how to take care of themselves and how to take care of the things God had given them. My sweet yet strong-willed kids had to learn some things the hard way. Learning to let go of control is one of the hardest but best lessons you can learn as a parent. You can't control them, and you can't control every situation. But you can teach them the tools necessary to live an abundant life through following Jesus and putting the right boundaries in place in their lives. Each kid will help guide you on the best way to raise them.

Breaking Generational Sin and Inequities

Where freedom also comes in parenting is when we realize there are some sin patterns affecting our lives and the lives of our children. There are some behaviors and lies that need to be broken off in the family line. There is such a range of generational patterns and sin, it is amazing at times to realize just how prevalent sin is within family lines but also how easy it is to break the pattern with the help of the Holy Spirit. The Bible speaks of generational issues that began early on in human history. Numbers 14:18 (ESV) tells us, "The LORD is slow to anger and abounding in steadfast love, forgiving iniquity and transgression, but he will by no means clear the guilty, visiting the iniquity of the fathers on the children, to the third and the fourth generation." The same general statement is repeated in Exodus 34:6–7. Does this still apply to us today? Absolutely. If you had told me four years ago about how generational patterns affect our lives and families, I would have laughed. But after living it and seeing the destruction that comes from not acknowledging God and instead walking further into sin, I can honestly say it is very real. Consequences of these sins last up to three or four generations.

But we do have an answer to the problems affecting us and our children. It is stated in Isaiah 53:5 (NIV), "But he was pierced for our transgressions, he was crushed for our iniquities; the punishment that brought us peace was upon him, and by his wounds we are healed." When we ask God for help and begin to untangle all the generational lies we have believed, he brings us into right relationship with him. He leads us into the renewal of our minds (Romans 12:2) to learn how to break off the old self and become a new self in Christ (2 Corinthians

5:17). The old is gone! We are whole, healed, and delivered when we come to salvation in Christ. The process of working out our salvation comes into play, and he graciously takes out all the generational yuck, the baggage we may have inherited from our forefathers, and replace it with his truths. We let go of the old life and take on a new wineskin. As born-again believers the effects of generational sin must be addressed, especially when it comes to parenting. Ask Jesus to set you free from any inherited bondage and recognize you are now grafted into God's family, with only blessings from your new family line.

An example of praying over how to break these generational iniquities would be the following prayer: "I honor my earthly father and mother, and all my ancestors of flesh and blood, adoptive parents or stepparents, but I utterly turn away from and renounce all their ungodly practices, sins, and iniquities. In the name of Jesus, I forgive all my ancestors for the effects of their sins on me and my children. Thank you, Father, for sending your only Son, the Lord Jesus Christ, to die in my place, to pay the penalty for my sins through his shed blood, and to bear the punishment for our sins and iniquities with his bruised and bleeding body on the cross of Calvary. I choose now to confess and take accountability for the sins through my family bloodlines back to the fourth generation, and to the tenth generation, and including my own, for sins known and unknown."[2]

Have Fun in Parenting

Becoming free from all the lies and sin patterns can lead your family into wholeness. One big lie I personally believed was that God did not have a sense of humor. He was this judgmental being in the sky who really did not know anything about love because he made life so hard. Boy was I wrong! Having kids shows you how to have fun, laugh, and find joy. God loves to laugh! He loves seeing His people restored to joy. Life is not all bad, and he does promise us we will see his goodness in the land of the living (Psalm 27:13–14). This includes having fun and enjoying your kids.

I see so many friends who are frustrated and angry or upset at their children a lot of the time. I was that parent at first. I did not understand why my children did not obey and believe me when I stated something the first time. I was so naïve. But when their little personalities grew and really started to show us how fun they were (my kids have some fun senses of humor!), it became apparent I was the stick-in-the-mud. I didn't know how to have fun. As God purposely slowed down our life, getting to spend time with my kids became such a gift. I learned how to encourage their imaginations, and I learned how to laugh with them and not be so hard on them and myself. God also showed me a different side of himself that few people talk about—his emotions. God has all the same emotions we have. He has joy, happiness, silliness, and a love of laughter! He's not this mean Father in the sky or the gentle Jesus pastors speak about in so many Western churches. He's actually all the fruit of the spirits combined into one being. He is gentleness, kindness, love, joy, peace, goodness, faithfulness, and patience. Can you imagine? At times, I cannot. Then he shows me his goodness through my children, and I know he's with me in the parenting journey.

    Have fun with your kids! They are such a wonderful gift, and even when it's rough, remember that God is with you leading you into freedom and wholeness in this part of your journey. While there is no perfect parent and no perfect child, there is a perfect God who wants to partner with you and raise some amazing kingdom-minded kids.

Scripture around Freedom in Parenting

- Proverbs 22:6 (ESV): "Train up a child in the way he should go; even when he is old he will not depart from it."

- Deuteronomy 11:19 (NKJV): "You shall teach them to your children, speaking of them when you sit in your house, when you walk by the way, when you lie down, and when you rise up."

- Exodus 34:6–7 (NLT): "The LORD passed in front of Moses, calling out, 'Yahweh! The LORD! The God of compassion and mercy! I am slow to anger and filled with unfailing love and faithfulness. I lavish unfailing love to a thousand generations. I forgive iniquity, rebellion, and sin. But I do not excuse the guilty. I lay the sins of the parents upon their children and grandchildren; the entire family is affected—even children in the third and fourth generations.'"

Unleash the Box

1. How has God made your children? What is unique about them, special about them?
2. How can you help your kids grow into kingdom-minded adults? What parenting style best suits your family?
3. Where might you be believing past lies and generational sins, causing your family not to walk in freedom?
4. How can you have fun with your kids? What are three fun things you can do with them this week?
5. Do you believe God has a sense of humor? If not, ask him to show you. What are you believing about God that is hindering your parenting journey? He wants to partner with you.

Prayer: Papa God, thank you for reminding us, we are all made in your image, empowered by your Spirit, and my children and I are part of your plan. Thank you for ideas and dreams which is beyond our ability. You always provide a plan that is purposeful and perfect. Help us to be excited!! In Jesus name, amen.

Chapter 8: Finding Freedom and Wholeness in Choices through Wisdom

> *Take God out of the box and allow Him to be the God that has no ending, the God that has power over everything, that speaks and creates, the God that is greater than sickness, the God that is greater than any need you may have and allow Him to supply the need. Give your situation, circumstances, and issues to God. Pray until you have a release of faith to move God.*
>
> —Carolyn Luke

Proverbs 16:2–3 (ESV) says, "All the ways of a man are pure in his own eyes, but the LORD weighs the spirit. Commit your work to the LORD, and your plans will be established."

When you read the news or listen to mainstream media, do you walk away feeling more empowered or more fearful? Do you take the time to investigate how world events line up with Scripture? Are you seeking wisdom? Wisdom is the beginning of all knowledge. Proverbs 9:10 (NIV) also says, "The fear of the LORD is the beginning of wisdom, and knowledge of the Holy One is understanding." Seeking wisdom and knowledge leads us to make better life choices. Wisdom comes through seeking the Lord on all fronts in life. If we aren't seeking his guidance, what are we seeking?

These are some of the questions which I have struggled with at times myself over the course of the last four years. Some choices are not wrong, and some choices are not right. We are to guard our hearts and, in doing so, increase in wisdom and understanding. We, the collective body of Christ, often elevate our behavior to be more important than God and allow our motives and choices to rule our lives. Our motives (what we value above all else) and our choices, in turn, are often revealed in our excuses and go straight to the heart. Ephesians 5:15–18 (NIV) encourages us, "Be very careful, then, how you live—not as unwise but as wise, making the most of every opportunity, because the days are evil. Therefore, do not be foolish, but understand what the Lord's will is. Do not get drunk on wine, which leads to debauchery. Instead, be filled with the Spirit." We are to live by the Spirit, which in turn helps us to live by wisdom. So many of us make poor behavioral choices because we have a poor view of God. We need to consider our testimony and how we reflect Christ more than we consider our rights. Living in a moment-by-moment relationship with Christ allows us to not be filled with things of this world but filled with the Spirit.

Seek Wisdom

How does someone go about seeking wisdom? Having wisdom enables us to make better choices that line up with God's Word and his journey for us. Pursuing knowledge and instruction with all our hearts will provide what we need to walk the blessed life with him. Below are some helpful reminders as you seek God's wisdom.

Study Scripture.

Studying Scripture is the gateway into understanding God, his heart for you, and supplying you with the knowledge of God. Proverbs 1:7 (NIV) says, "The fear of the LORD is the beginning of knowledge, but fools despise wisdom and instruction." Because so many people do not have a healthy fear of the Lord, they fear man instead, which takes God out of his rightful place in their lives. When we do this, we relegate God to a box and make him small. The God in Proverbs talks about how to gain wisdom and how to make life choices. Why not ask him today how you can build wisdom into your life?

Proverbs 2:5 (NIV) reminds us, "Then you will understand the fear of the LORD and find the knowledge of God." The knowledge of God involves knowing God as a person and knowing what he is teaching us. Scripture is filled with this notion of God as a person. As Philippians 3:10–11 (NIV) says, "I want to know Christ—yes, to know the power of his resurrection and participation in his sufferings, becoming like him in his death, and so, somehow, attaining to the resurrection from the dead." Knowing Christ happens through personal experience by posturing your heart toward Him, transforming your entire person.

Build your house.

Proverbs 9:1 (NIV) tells us, "Wisdom has built her house." In this verse wisdom is personified as a woman who at some point was in the process of building her home, or foundation. In other words, growing in wisdom is a process, and at some point, we arrive at the end of the process. To build wisdom is to "forsake foolishness and live, and go in the way of understanding," as Proverbs 9:6 (NKJV) says. The process includes studying diligently in the context of whatever gifting or talents the Lord has given you. Take it upon yourself to do this; take responsibility for it yourself. Pursue knowledge and instruction with all your heart, for in doing so you will learn what you need to learn to walk the blessed life with God.

This also means the opposite of wisdom is foolishness, and it has not built its house. If you are wise, you will build your house, and if you are a fool, you will not build your house. What does this mean? We often neglect to build our own house. We take care of other people, but do we take care of ourselves? We care for other people's health; do we care for our own? We watch out for other people's financial interests at work and other places, but do we diligently care for our own finances at home? Do we prepare for emergencies at our own house?

Taking care of the things God has entrusted to you is a sign of wisdom. Build your own house. Don't stop taking care of others and serving the Lord but be sure to take care of your own home and those inside that house.

Ask for his help.

In the books of Psalms and Isaiah, there are many verses that speak to God as our ever-present help. Do you know him that way? Psalm 46:1–3 (NIV) reminds us, "God is our refuge and strength, an ever-present help in trouble. Therefore, we will not fear, though the earth gives way and the mountains fall into the heart of the sea, though its waters roar and foam and the mountains quake with their surging." In a recent article on wisdom, I found the following extremely helpful: "You will often find that My help is prepared and positioned for you before you even ask for it. You will experience the reality of 'Before you call, I will answer.' So call upon Me any time you need help, and it shall be given to you. Say My name, the name of Jesus, whenever you need Me and I will manifest Myself to you. My help is for you. It is not just for someone else. My help is for you, for I see your every cry and I am the One catching your tears. You have no idea how close to Me you are, and you have no idea how close to you I am. *I am in you, with you, and for you; never forget it!*" (emphasis mine).[1]

Expect God to show up.

If you are going to receive anything from the Lord, you must expect to receive. According to the Bible, if you have given your life to Jesus, then you are entitled to every blessing God gave to Abraham because you are grafted into Abraham's covenant with God through Christ. Remind God you are a part of the covenant He gave Abraham because you are grafted in through Christ. Present all the blessings God gave to Abraham back to him in prayer and insist in faith upon receiving them yourself (Hebrews 11:6). You will be shocked at what God does in response to this study of Abraham, and in response to praying the blessings of Abraham back to Him.[2]

The Parable of the Ten Virgins

This parable in Matthew 25 has multiple meanings. It is a parable around watching and waiting for our Bridegroom, Jesus, to return; it's also about wisdom and provision. The story includes five wise virgins and five foolish virgins. They are taking their lamps and going out to meet their bridegroom. These ten virgins are the bridesmaids, the ones responsible for preparing the bride to meet the bridegroom. The lamps are torches that consist of a long pole with oil-drenched rags at the top. These were used for outdoor ceremonies. In the parable, the foolish ones took their lamps but did not take any oil with them. The wise, however, took oil in jars along with their lamps. The bridegroom was a long time in coming, and they all became drowsy and fell asleep. As the story goes, the cry rang out that the bridegroom had returned, and everyone was to come out to meet Him. The foolish virgins asked the wise virgins for oil for their lamps since their lamps were going out. But the wise virgins told the foolish ones to go get their own oil. While the foolish ones were gone, the wise virgins went into the wedding banquet and the door was closed. The famous verse in this story is Matthew 25:12 (CEB): "But he [the bridegroom] replied, 'I tell you the truth, I don't know you.'"

    What does all this represent? The oil is your relationship with the Spirit. Are you filling up your own lamp with oil, or are you filling up everyone else's lamp and neglecting your own? We are to spend time with the Father to have our lamps filled and be ready for his return. This requires wisdom—having the wisdom to know where to spend our time, where to place our values, and how to be in the world but not of it. We are also not responsible for others' faith, and we are not to enable others who are not doing their own work. Nurturing our relationship with the Lord is equivalent to preserving the oil in our lamp. As we wait on the Lord and keep watch for his return, he tells us it's going to be long, and he will be late, a long time in coming. In the waiting, it is our responsibility to get to know God and fill our oil jars.

Wisdom is seeking the kingdom of God first and allowing everything else to work itself out with the help of God. In James 1:5 (NIV), we're told, "If any of you lacks wisdom, you should ask God, who gives generously to all without finding fault, and it will be given to you." Wisdom is not just acquired information but practical insight with spiritual implications. It comes from relationship with God. In filling your oil jars with God's wisdom, you will be ready for his return. We aren't to be conformed to this world but to build our house, "for the LORD gives wisdom; from his mouth come knowledge and understanding (Proverbs 2:6 NIV). How are you filling your oil jar? Are you asking the Lord for wisdom on when and how to live your life? In the waiting, can you trust the Lord for provision, clarity, and integrity?

Word from a Dear Friend on Choices

As I walked out an exceedingly difficult season in my marriage, which ultimately ended in divorce, God had placed some incredibly special and unique people in my life. One year of walking this arduous path proved to be a season when I had to make several choices. Spending time alone with the Lord, going on walks by myself, worshipping, and seeking His face was the only way I got through this time. God presented multiple choices before me, allowing different paths and answers to my struggles.

In our struggles is when we grow closest to God because at times he is all we have. As you read the words below from my friend, know they are from someone who has been completely healed of multiple sclerosis. She had a choice laid before her—to surrender or to continue in the yuck. Choices are not easy, but when they are lined up with wisdom, taking each step of obedience is sweeter than any circumstances swirling around us.

As I was out walking one day during this season, my friend texted me this:

> The Holy Spirit said, "Set your eyes on things above." This reminded her of the scripture passage he'd given her in the middle of the night. He used it to explain why he was not going to heal her all at once. He has been giving me my whole testimony little by little in answer to my prayer that I don't want any word to come out of my mouth in my ministry that isn't given by him, so I understood last night why he brought it. So excited he is revealing himself afresh to you, Heather. His Word tells us that if we ask, seek or knock, he will respond. We must be ready to respond with a quiet and contrite heart to hear what he wants to tell us. Keep leaning in. Continue to pursue him with an unrelenting passion for the power of his presence. He will give you

that desire of your heart because it's also the desire of his. Holy Spirit asked this question to me through my friend Tina, "Will you let go of the timing of your future and embrace the place I have you? Trust me. I have you right where you are supposed to be."

The verses given to her, presented below, were about the law of possessing the land, as recorded in the book of Numbers. Kicking out all the unwelcome "inhabitants" in her land (the spirits, beliefs, and lies she had made partnerships with) gave her healing and freedom. It was choice.

Then the LORD spoke to Moses in the plains of Moab by the Jordan across from Jericho, saying, "Say to the children of Israel, 'When you cross the Jordan into the land of Canaan, then you shall drive out all the inhabitants of the land before you and destroy all their sculpted images, and destroy all their cast idols and completely eliminate all their [idolatrous] high places, and you shall take possession of the land and live in it, for I have given the land to you to possess. You shall inherit the land by lot according to your families; to the large tribe you shall give a larger inheritance, and to the small tribe you shall give a smaller inheritance. Wherever the lot falls to any man, that shall be [the location of] his [inheritance]. According to the tribes of your fathers (ancestors) you shall inherit. But if you do not drive out the inhabitants of the land from before you, then those you let remain of them will be like pricks in your eyes and like thorns in your sides, and they will attack you in the land in which you live. And as I [the LORD] planned to do to them, so I will do to you.'" (Numbers 33:50–56 AMP)

Taking Back Your Land

One thing people don't realize is that sin, inequity, and other desires we seek to fulfill outside of God create partnerships with the enemy (Satan). We have an enemy who is real and who seeks to kill, steal, and destroy. The Bible says he walks around like a roaring lion (1 Peter 5:8). So how do we guard against making these partnerships with the enemy? We go through the inner healing process, allowing the Holy Spirit to untangle these places (aka our land or our home) where we have given over pieces of who we are and made partnerships with something unholy. Sin is seeking a replacement for God, filling a void with something else other than Jesus, having our own way, and thinking our way is better than the way of Jesus.

An example of this is Solomon using God's blessings to indulge every sinful desire. God intends for his kindness to lead us to repent (Romans 2:4). God's grace "teaches us to say 'No' to ungodliness . . . and to live self-controlled, upright and godly lives" (Titus 2:12 NIV). His amazing grace and the Holy Spirit teach us how to come into right relationship and pray through all the places where we have allowed the enemy to take up territory in our hearts. These "landing strips" are places where we have said yes to the enemy, thinking his ways are better, and saying no to what God has to offer.

An example of this for me occurred when I was dealing with the spirits of anger, control, and comparison. Through the house exercise described in chapter 2, the Holy Spirit guided me through inner healing prayer, dealing with what was at play in my inner being. These were the spirits (don't be freaked out by this word) I was dealing with, which had kept me tied up in bondage. I tried so desperately to control everything in my life, I was at the end of my rope. Controlling left me desperate, tired, and weary from the constant need to oversee it all. Comparison left me wanting to be other people, not happy with my life, and wanting something different. When we prayed with the Holy Spirit, he healed me of these two spirits instantaneously! The spirits were gone, and I was completely free of them. I knew this when I got together with extended family, and they told of us their amazing lake house purchase. I was so excited for them! In the past, I would have been judgmental, thinking unkind thoughts, and just tied up in the what-ifs. However, this time I was completely free from the weight of comparison and truly happy for the blessing the Lord had given them with their new home.

Satan wants to keep us in the old life of being undelivered. This is where Satan wants us—tied up in our thoughts, self-centered, and not walking with God daily. If this is you, there are prayers you can walk through to find deliverance. God wants you delivered, healed, and whole. That's what salvation means—healed and whole. When we meet with God and ask the Holy Spirit into this process, God brings about healing in such a way there are no other words than miraculous. Being healed from comparison and the other spirits has brought about such amazing life transformation that only God could do. The Holy Spirit isn't your weird uncle; He is alive and living inside you when you come to Christ through the saving grace of Jesus. If you want to know what is possible in this life, this side of heaven, invite the Holy Spirit to search you and know your heart (Psalm 139:23). Ask him to show you where you have made partnerships with the enemy and to help you come into healing. It's possible, but only through faith in Jesus Christ can you come into true healing and freedom. He will walk you through it if you ask him for his help. Psalm 86:11 (NIV) tells us, "Teach me your way, LORD, that I may rely on your faithfulness; give me an undivided heart, that I may fear your name."

Scripture around Freedom in Choices through Wisdom

- Proverbs 1:7 (ISV): "The fear of the LORD is the beginning of knowledge, but fools despise wisdom and discipline."

- Proverbs 2:5 (NIV): "Then you will understand the fear of the LORD and find the knowledge of God."

- Proverbs 4:7 (CSB): "Wisdom is supreme—so get wisdom. And whatever else you get, get understanding."

- Proverbs 9:9–10 (TLV): "Instruct a wise man and he will be wiser still. Teach a righteous man and he will increase in learning. The fear of Adonai [the Lord] is the beginning of wisdom and knowledge of the Holy One is understanding."

- James 1:5–6 (NIV): "If any of you lacks wisdom, you should ask God, who gives generously to all without finding fault, and it will be given to you. But when you ask, you must believe and not doubt, because the one who doubts is like a wave of the sea, blown and tossed by the wind."

- Philippians 3:10–11 (NIV): "I want to know Christ—yes, to know the power of his resurrection and participation in his sufferings, becoming like him in his death, and so, somehow, attaining to the resurrection from the dead."

Unleash the Box

1. Where in your life are you not believing and asking God for wisdom?
2. Are you doubting God will show up? Or are you living from a place of control, unable to see above your circumstances? If so, ask God to show up. Ask Him to help you see above what's going on around you. Then expect Him to do what he says.
3. God wants to build your house from the inside out into something amazing. Do you ever find yourself building others' houses and neglecting your own? Elaborate your answer.
4. Is your lamp filled? Are you ready for the return of the Bridegroom? How can you fill your lamp today?
5. Where to do you place your trust – in God or in man? Do you have a healthy fear of him? What is standing in the way of maintaining a healthy fear of God? Fearing (reverence/awe) is the beginning of wisdom.

6. Where have you given access to the enemy? Pray with the Holy Spirit to take away anything which isn't of him and give back the truths of His heart.

7. The greatness of God's grace demands a greater response than mere outward conformity. God wanted Solomon's whole heart. David demonstrated how imperfect people can display true "integrity of heart and uprightness" (1 Kings 9:4 ESV). God promises his heart to his people and asks for our whole hearts in return. What might be stopping you from asking God for wisdom to enter your heart? Can you choose to believe he will give his whole heart in return?

Prayer: Papa, show us how to walk in your wisdom. Your wisdom is not of this world, but of your kingdom. Help us in our unbelief and doubt so we may know you fully. Guide us to build our house of wisdom with you. Fill up our lamps with your oil, and give us insight to know what is of you and what is of this world. Lead, guide, and direct our footsteps. In Jesus's name, amen.

Chapter 9: Finding Freedom and Wholeness from Religious and Poverty Spirits

Whenever we accept limitations, we put God in a box and ourselves in a box. God does not want to be in a box, and He does not want us in a box or confined with limited thinking and limited beliefs.

—Dennis Funderberg

Religion is a very divisive topic. Religion means belief in, worship of, or obedience to a supernatural power or powers considered to be divine or to have control of human destiny any formal or institutionalized expression of such belief the Christian religion. It can be either a source of joy or a source of discontentment and pain. What has been interesting in the last few years is the unlearning of what it means to be in relationship with God. What is taught in Western churches is not the gospel. The American gospel is incomplete—it is about being saved and not discipled. Jesus is not an à la carte menu, as some would have you imagine, where you get to pick the aspects of him you want to follow. He is a complete, triune God in relationship with himself, and he longs to have that kind of intimate relationship with each of his followers.

Coming into a Right Relationship with God

What do you believe about the Bible? Do you see it as a collection of stories, imagery, spiritual realities, or actual realities and real people? What do you believe is true? The Bible provides the context in which to live. If God—Father, Son, and Holy Spirit—is alive and truly a person, then he also lives outside the pages of the Bible speaking to us and helping us as we live our lives.

Stories give life to us. We are a part of a broader story, and those stories invite us to know the God who is in the Bible. The Bible is where we meet our heavenly Father, through a broader, unfolding story. It helps each of us to know where we fall in the narrative. There is history behind the pre-cross Christ and the story of a risen, victorious Savior. If we believe in a risen, victorious Savior, then the victory is ours! Claim it!

As you look around at the bigger picture and the world, you will notice we are a world at war. There is a bigger plan at play between good and evil. You get to choose which side of history you want to be a part of in this bigger picture. So, ask yourself, what side do I fall on? Will I choose God or Satan? Satan wants to keep all of us shackled in religion and legalism to the point we are powerless and unable to live out the victory given to us by victorious Christ. This is where we end up compromising our freedom and letting darkness, or sin, in. We make peace treaties with the enemy on different things where we let the enemy have land. Sin is, in part, seeking to get our needs met apart from God. We want things that are outside the nature of God. Sin is motivated by the heart leading to behaviors we regret; sin leads to consequences with each other and with God. Something always changes because of our sin. When God convicts us at the heart and root issue of our sin, we become aware. Consequences of sin give the enemy legal permission in our life.

By the gracious and loving nature of God, he wants to clean up our hearts. Psalm 51:10 (NIV) says, "Create in me a pure heart, O God, and renew a steadfast spirit within me." When you think of the prodigal son, he had greed in his heart causing him to leave his home and family. Likewise, when we sin, we are choosing to live apart from God as well. We make a choice to go our own way and not accept God's fullness. This leads to partnering with the world and allowing the enemy into our lives. God will convict our hearts, but will we move toward God in repentance or continue in our sin? In the story of the one sheep versus the ninety-nine (Luke 15:1–7), he calls and persists until he finds that one. The Lord invites us to repentance and cleansing from sin, to be whole and free when we receive salvation.

What Gospel Did You Receive?

What salvation message did you receive? What is it you needed? What did it ask of you? The American gospel, the message commonly taught in many U.S. churches every Sunday, is incomplete because it only speaks to one piece of the puzzle—salvation for sin. It does not speak about the gospel of the kingdom. When I first heard of Sozo, inner healing, I was skeptical. This concept is not taught widely in the American church and as God asked me to step into this, it became apparent I knew nothing about the gospel of the kingdom.

Sozo in the Greek means salvation. In the Bible it is used multiple times in different ways to describe different scenarios of healing and deliverance in the Bible.

Abundantly Supplied

Salvation not only means forgiveness of sins but also includes physical healing, deliverance, and financial prosperity too. Many in the modern church have interpreted salvation only to mean forgiveness of sins, but that is a misrepresentation of what the Lord did. Forgiveness of our sins is certainly the centerpiece, and no one is minimizing the importance of the cross at all. However, at the same time Christ died to purchase our redemption from sin, he also freed us from sickness, disease, depression, and poverty.[1]

Here is where people get persuaded into thinking along the lines of the American gospel. They think it is not a Holy Spirit experience or that the Holy Spirit is some weird cousin no one talks about. They think the Holy Spirit just hangs around, and we are subject to a fallen world but surely we are saved for eternity. Guess what? We are citizens of God's kingdom—heaven on earth! We are not to wait on heaven because heaven is available today! God initiates the relationship with us, then we do our part by surrendering our life to the call of God. When we surrender to the healing power of Jesus and renounce and repent of our sin (lay down our life), all his inheritance—Jesus himself—becomes ours.

When we surrender to the call on our lives by God, he gets to work at renewing our minds. Our minds need to be rewired, refreshed, and renewed with the truth of who God truly is—a three-in-one God. Romans 12:2 (NIV) reminds us, "Do not conform to the pattern of this world, but be transformed by the renewing of your mind. Then you will be able to test and approve what God's will is—his good, pleasing and perfect will." We are to be transformed! Getting as close as you can to the real thing will enable you to never miss a thing. He is the one who is true. If we are to call on the one who can do all things, how come our experience does not line up with Scripture? If my experience does not agree with Scripture, am I going to come before God and ask God to reveal what is keeping me from abundance? Abundant living is possible because God withholds no good gift! As my inner healing counselor, Kelly, has explained to me, abundant living comes from abiding in the presence of our most beloved King of Kings!

A Different Worldview

Saying that all things are from God misuses Romans 8:28 (NIV), which says, "He uses all things for our good." In other words, God can use any circumstance, good or bad, but that doesn't mean all circumstances come from his hand. When you look more closely at the story of the prodigal son, for example, you see where the son chose to walk away and how his reality became eating pig slop. He finally realizes that everything is waiting for him at his father's house. The father accepts him back, no questions, and instead simply rejoices in the return of his lost son. God made good of the prodigal son's situation, but he didn't cause it. We all need to stand with God on the truth of Romans 8:28 in order to understand where we have let the enemy in and how our beliefs aren't lining up with his truth. We must also remember who God is in the spiritual realm, as outlined below.

Spiritual Realm

God is three persons: Father, Son, and Holy Spirit. There is specificity to each person in the Godhead. The main thing to remember is the Godhead is based on relationship. When you delve into Psalm 23, you see a caring relationship displayed through rest, provision, and peace. This goes against how God is portrayed in works-based or performance religion. Performance religion says we serve and give according to the demands of the world because it's our call as Christians. In reality, the Bible speaks to the importance of being in relationship first with the Father, then serving out of love for Him. Ask yourself how you got off the right path with him? Scriptural truths show us that he wants to help us move toward him. As he draws us in, he reveals who he is and his nature to us. He wants our hearts, and he wants us to long to be near him, not just obey him. He envelops us in his love, and we choose whether or not to walk close to him. He is unchanging, and he cares about what is going on inside us. None of this relationship is produced in our own strength. When we try to work out our relationship with God on our own, that is behavior management, which produces more bondage, in contrast with a true relationship with him where we don't have to perform in order to be his child. As stated earlier in chapter 3, God wants truth in our innermost being above all else. As Psalm 51:6 (WEB) reminds us, "Behold, you desire truth in the inward parts. You teach me wisdom in the inmost place." Proverbs 20:27 (ESV) adds, "The spirit of man is the lamp of the LORD, searching all his innermost parts." Truth in our innermost beings, is not produced in our own strength and self-effort. It is from knowing the One who is unchanging! He wants our hearts.

The Triune God is a God who exists as three coequal, coeternal persons. God the Father, God the Son, and God the Holy Spirit remain distinct. Yet they exist in perfect, indivisible unity with one mind in all things:

1. God the Father chiefly planned creation and salvation.
2. God the Son, the Lord Jesus Christ, chiefly achieved these plans.
3. God the Holy Spirit chiefly proclaims these works in order to call people to faith in Christ.

1. **Father/Yahweh/God—First Person of the Triune God**

There are multiple barriers when it comes to understanding and coming into right standing with the Lord. We relate to him as our earthly Father. Our earthly fathers are well-intentioned but often misguided in their actions. We miss out on aspects of our relationship with God when we relate to him as our earthly Father. Another barrier occurs when we consider God to be generic and attribute everything to Jesus. God is not generic but very much a person who exists outside in addition to within Scripture. A third barrier to knowing Yahweh God is overly focusing on the distinctions between the New Testament and the Old Testament. But God exists in both parts of the Bible. He is the beginning and the end: "I am the Alpha and the Omega, the First and the Last, the Beginning and the End" (Revelation 22:13 NIV). Understanding the characteristics of God can help removing the barriers to coming into right relationship with Him.

2. **Jesus Christ, God the Son—Second Person of the Triune God**

Jesus came to earth to die for our sins. This amazing truth transcends all time and space continuums. Because of his victorious sacrifice, we have direct access to the Father. The veil was torn, giving us direct access to the Father (Praise Yahweh!). Jesus made the way for us, and we should not miss it! Throughout the book of John, Jesus did only what the Father was already doing: he modeled what is possible for us to have in a right relationship with the Father. According to Acts 2:22 (NIV), "Jesus of Nazareth was a man accredited by God to you by miracles, wonders and signs, which God did among you through him, you yourselves know." A common barrier to rightly positioning Jesus is that we assign or associate God with Jesus, which prevents us from acknowledging and understanding who Jesus really is. Jesus lived by the power of the Spirit. Jesus—the way, the truth, and the life—is not the end; he is the way. Jesus paid the price, and he tore the veil, which gave us direct access to the Father.

Jesus gave us victory, so now we can live everything he modeled. Jesus modeled for us how to live in right relationship with the Father. God came and lived a life we could not have lived and stood in the gap for us. He gives us the exchanged life, where He died in our place, which prevents us from having to pay the cost for our sinful lives. We often stop short and fail to step into the life he wants for us. The ultimate truth is that we are in relationship with the Father, and Jesus closes every gap. We can trade in our holey umbrella. He is our refuge and covering, and we can stand in a raging storm and be dry. All because of his life he sacrificed for us.

When we walk with Jesus in this exchanged life, he along peels away the things we are too comfortable with. By taking his hand alone, we step into his purposes for us. Order matters to God. Jesus comes into our lives, clean up the inside, and turn us loose to walk out heaven on earth. As he turns us loose, what does it mean to be an effective witness? There are certain traits of a godly person. Do you dance with the Spirit and live that way? Where do we fall short in the story God is writing? John 16:7 (ESV) displays Jesus's words, and his heart for us, before his ascension and resurrection: "Nevertheless, I tell you the truth: it is to your advantage that I go away, for if I do not go away, the Helper will not come to you. But if I go, I will send him to you."

3. Holy Spirit—Third Person of the Triune God

The Holy Spirit is described as a dove (see Matthew 3:16, Mark 1:10, Luke 3:22, and John 1:32). God's kingdom, through the Holy Spirit, is on earth now and not something we wait for or hope for once we die. It is present and powered through the Holy Spirit in our lives. Most people operate from a standpoint that the Holy Spirit was but is no more. They assume the Holy Spirit was only around for a time, which is called cessation of the Spirit. The Holy Spirit is often compared to the weird uncle. People tend to fear any chaotic, uncomfortable, new age, immature, or fleshly representation of the Holy Spirit. But Spirit without truth does not work. He is God of Father and of Spirit. If we continue to walk with God, we need to invite the Holy Spirit into our internal lives to clean out the junk. We are invited to live by the Spirit, where the Spirit always initiates, prompts us, guides us, serves God, translates, and intercedes for us, and keeps us under his protection.

When we come to understand the power of the Spirit, we begin to see how each component of our lives—our vocation, hobbies, relationships, etc.—plays a part in the bigger story. The Bible is the true and inherent Word of God. We are to relate to it as a living guidebook from God. It is a powerful tool for us to come to know who God is and our life purpose. God uses the Spirit to show us where in the Bible we need to focus when he is guiding us. If your experience does not agree with Scripture, you can come before God and ask the Holy Spirit to reveal what is keeping you from abundance.

When you get as close as you can to the real thing (God himself), you realize you will never miss a thing. The Holy Spirit initiates intimacy with the Lord, which empowers you to walk out your purpose, says, Kelly, inner healer counselor.

Common Barriers to Walking in Right Relationship with God

We all have belief barriers meaning we all have something immaterial that obstructs or impedes the Trinity from working in us. Each of these barriers keep us from walking the freedom Jesus died to give us. When you start to deconstruct these barriers with the help of the Holy Spirit, you come into a better understanding of what it means to follow him.

Barrier 1

Barrier 1 is an outward display of religion. Many people walk this out by believing if they behave a certain way it will ensure their salvation. God does not look at our performance or outward appearance. He looks at the heart. As 1 Samuel 16:7 (NIV) tells us, "But the LORD said to Samuel, "Do not consider his appearance or his height, for I have rejected him. The LORD does not look at the things people look at. People look at the outward appearance, but the LORD looks at the heart." It is not our job to judge people's hearts by acting like our way of Christianity is better than that of others. Too many people take one verse and do not hold it in the right tension; instead, they use it to judge the actions and behaviors of others. Consider how Jesus engaged in conflict; he never shied away from truth. Behavior management denies our spirit the ability to be human, to engage in conflict honestly and openly. God lives in the tension, in the middle where we can be our integrated, whole selves.

Barrier 2

Barrier 2 is thinking that because we go to church, we are doing okay. God says we *are* the church! We are each a child of God simply by hearing his voice and walking closely with him. Ask God to open your eyes and tune your ears to his truth. Many churches today are like wolves in sheep's clothing only preaching one message. If we're in tune with God, our hearts and ears will know the difference. We know what real love, joy, and peace (not fake) feels like. The Western church tends to portray Jesus as Flat Jesus, as if he was a one-dimensional person, always tolerant and always selfless. This is a false portrayal of who he is and does not align with the life he came to give us. He was direct, candid, abrupt, and harsh with the Pharisees, angry at those who profited from the gospel, and never pushy, as when he allowed the young rich ruler to walk away.

How can we walk out being the church?

A. We can be imitators of Christ. Currently the world is influencing the church rather than the other way around. The frantic pace of life and technology, the level of numbness we tolerate, our performance expectations, and our behavior orientation all mimic the world. Jesus came to clean and change us on the inside. What did the disciples do? They followed along with Jesus, and it was a big deal for them to do so. The dirt on Jesus's shoes would be on them. If our kids choose to imitate us, are they supposed to be doormats with no sense of self or warriors and martyrs who stand up for what is right? Imitating Christ means standing up for the truth even when it costs us everything.

B. If we walk and live as Christ walked and lived, we will live the way it is possible in the Spirit. Wholeness and abundance are possible through the Holy Spirit, but our choices have consequences. In many Western churches today, emotional and relational health has eroded. Scripture says that by their love you will know the disciples of Jesus (John 13:35). Do people know you as an imitator of the life of Christ? The upside-down kingdom brings heaven to earth, meaning to follow Him means to walk with him and live as he lived.

C. Our identity in Christ was fully paid for in Christ. We identify with the victorious Christ who took all of it and said, "It is finished!" (John 19:30 NIV). He is alive—the power of darkness is under our feet! Sickness, evil, and affliction are all works of darkness. Most believers no longer recognize, or fail to realize, we serve a victorious Savior where the power of darkness is under our feet even in the realm of health. Those he set free are free indeed! *Sozo*, or salvation, means whole, healed, and delivered. According to Matthew 12:43–45 (NIV), "When an impure spirit comes out of a person, it goes through arid places seeking rest and does not find it. Then it says, 'I will return to the house I left.' When it arrives, it finds the house unoccupied, swept clean and put in order. Then it goes and takes with it seven other spirits more wicked than itself, and they go in and live there. And the final condition of that person is worse than the first. That is how it will be with this wicked generation." Jesus talks about someone not being delivered and allowing more spirits to come back if the root isn't healed. Jesus comes in and heals at the root. Where has the enemy come to live in your life? We must cleanse the footholds. Disciples tasted miracles and walked with Jesus, and the Bible says the same Spirit that lives in him (and lived with them) also lives in us.

D. What does living in victory mean for us? He lived a perfect life; he was victorious over the cross. Christ has already paid the price. We are to live in his victory! We must not settle for what is not real, like the false or incomplete religion presented in many churches. We have access to the true life, and we're invited to live with him. The Holy Spirit guides us and, as a result, if we're obedient, produces in us the fruit of the Spirit.

Barrier 3

Barrier 3 involves assuming that a right relationship with God is only available for certain people. Coming into a right relationship with God points to God's desire to connect with people and his willingness to make that connection happen. Walking the right relationship with the Father is available to all of us now, not just a certain few. We live from that place of victory because of Jesus. Guidance comes from God and will follow the Spirit. Part of the process of coming into a right relationship with God requires that we also come into right relationship with ourselves. In Genesis, the Triune God made man in his image. God is relational, and so are we. You also are body, mind, and emotions, and you have a relationship with yourself. The movie *Inside Out* is still one of my favorite depictions of how our inner self can become our outer reality. To move into wholeness and freedom with the Lord, you must own the relationship you have with yourself. He made you, he desires relationship with you, and he longs for you to see yourself the way he sees you (Psalm 139).

What does having a relationship with yourself look like from God's perspective? Here are some questions to consider:

A. What relationship do you have with yourself? We all need to rest, eat, acknowledge our emotions (pain, joy, sorrow, happiness, etc.), and recognize when we feel tired. Are you meeting those needs? What about your thoughts? What is the loudest voice in your heard that you're listening to? What thoughts in your head didn't originate with you? Where did they originate instead? Take captive every thought. As Romans 12:2 (AMP) commands, "And do not be conformed to this world [any longer with its superficial values and customs], but be transformed and progressively changed [as you mature spiritually] by the renewing of your mind [focusing on godly values and ethical attitudes], so that you may prove [for yourselves] what the will of God is, that which is good and acceptable and perfect [in His plan and purpose for you]."

B. Are you fully integrated between your heart and emotions because you are taking care of yourself? Do you deny any part of your body by serving outward voices versus inward needs?

C. Whom or what are you serving? Christianity says to deny yourself, or to live a life of love and service. The fruit of a healthy, vibrant believer is living as one who is loved. Most people who claim to be Christians are white-washed tombs and are dead on the inside. They do not value the heart, failing to heed the warning in Proverbs 4:23 (NLT): "Guard your heart above all else." Your outward disposition is an indicator of a righteous person. This means the power and fruit of the Spirit flow from an inner reality of being in right relationship with God. Love your God and love your neighbor as you love yourself. This is the natural overflow of a loved heart.

D. Do you know how to treat yourself? Do you always push past yourself by saying yes to everything instead of no to things that are unhealthy for you? Who do you believe you are? Who is he for you? As my inner healing counselor, Kelly, once reminded me, Jesus felt pain deeply, but he knew his death was not the end of the story! What does abundant life look like to you? Throw off anything that hinders. Fall into pace with your Father, which will look very different than the pace of the world.

Asking God to reshape your thinking by removing these barriers to belief will open a world of possibilities before you. He loves you so much and wants to bring his love to fruition in your life.

Victory from the Spirit of Poverty

As the Lord continued to unravel my old belief systems and bring me closer to him, it became very apparent I was dealing with the spirit of poverty. A spirit of poverty is closely tied to the spirit of religion discussed above. When we partner with the enemy in different ways, we end up compromising with sin and not living the abundant life Jesus calls us to. The excerpt below is from Dennis Funderburg at Five Crown Ministries from the *Jesus Is Still Jesus* podcast. His podcast is about coming into right relationship with God and seeking the Father's heart above all else. Hope the words below bless you and bring you into the freedom he so desires for your life:

In Exodus 3, Moses has an encounter with the burning bush and God told Moses the Israelites would plunder the Egyptians and take those riches. Moses came back to God and asked what if they do not believe me? Please send someone else and God commissioned Aaron to help Moses. God was trying to break the spirit of poverty over Moses.

The poverty spirit is a spirit which comes to hinder believers in Christ. It is a state of being inferior, keeping you trapped in a lower state of being which keeps you from living an ascended lifestyle. There are types of poverty such as poverty to imagination, courage, how you view yourself or your will (self-perception). It keeps you from being all you are called to be and accepting limitations. Whenever we accept limitations, we put God in a box and ourselves in a box.

God does not want to be in a box, and He does not want us in a box or confined with limited thinking and limited beliefs.

Poverty is a place of where you are constantly being governed by lack. Poverty comes when the lack itself governs you based on current resources at that time. It keeps you stagnant from moving forward, not allowing us to step forward in faith to meet God's provision. When God gives us a promise there is a process, we go to which will lead to provision. It is always promises – process – provision.

The enemy tries to stop us in the progress of the process and provision is a step ahead of us which is faith. Action in love will take you through the process so you can walk into God's provision. Why have you been stuck in a season so long? Because poverty works with a spirit of confusion. The spirit of confusion throws you off balance because those spirits are working against you. Do not let the process of a promise led you to poverty when destined for provision. Provision is always one step ahead of a poverty mindset.

God has not called anyone to scrap along the bottom. 2 Corinthians 9:8 "And God is able to bless you abundantly, so that in all things at all times, having all that you need, you will abound in every good work." Giving your heart, your future, your past, and your everything allows you to abound through the love and intimacy of your relationship with Him. I accept this promise and walk out to provision. I have a part in this of worship, adoration and allowing my character, discipline, my humility, patience to be subjected to God's will so I can inherit what He has for me and bless and give back to Him (honor Him).

2 Peter 1:3 "His divine power has given us everything we need for a godly life through our knowledge of him who called us by his own glory and goodness." His divine power given to us is for a godly

life. What is the intent of your life (heart)? The in and out of your innermost being? We want to serve God, but also want to appear to be important. Do not measure yourself by your externals! You will be attacked by the poverty spirit. Do not measure your life by your bank balance, resources, your environment, your past, or opinions of other people. Long before people had an opinion about you, God said who you are. All opinions become irrelevant. Be defined inwardly by God's permission and promises! If you receive a promise from God, it is a permission. You have permission to take hold of it. Take hold of what you have now and steward it. Your personal assumptions will defeat you or inspire you. If you opinion is based on what God says you are – you will have a natural desire to be that person – more like Jesus.

We are to contend in warfare from promises! If you have a promise from God it allows you to see with a different lens. Warfare reveals inheritance! Satan has a limited budget. He is organized because he must be with who he attacks and when and he cannot release every spirit on every person. His goal is to create the most damage which keeps people from inheriting. He puts up roadblocks – He attacks where we are supposed to be. His goal is keeping you from inheriting promises (Satan's goal) the only way Satan can defeat you! When you believe the lies you become a shadow of your own possibilities. Repent of the lies and break out of that poverty mind-set!

Prophetic word: Beloved, it is my desire for you to have the same relationship with me that I do with Jesus. Your heart to be filled with the harmony of Heaven. Immerse with the Trinity when you fellowship with us, you walk in the land of promise, lead you out of the lies of lack and into my intentions. In my love there is no stress, no strain, and no struggle. Let the pressure of peace inside you be greater than the pressure of stress on the outside of you. Your inheritance is so vast, there is promises hidden in your heart, promises next to the problems you have in life, learn how to be confident in me and your joy will be complete. Live in my delight for you – it will lead to training, discipline, and development. Exchange your chaos for my Kingdom. My discipline is not to call you out on your behavior, but to call you up into your identity. Designed you to be different – your rejections were a sign you belong to me. The world rejects what intimidates, and they do not understand. As I gave wealth to the Israelites, so I will give to you. If you show up, I will show off. Open every door man would not. I have big dreams for you. Be filled with hope and the expectation of goodness. The less you control the more I will move!![2]

Walking into freedom after unraveling the religious and poverty spirits in my life, moved me into abundance. Resetting my mind on the things above such as grace, mercy, love and kindness, allowed me to see my circumstances through a new view. This view gave me a new appreciation for the work and life set before me. Ask God to fill you with his hope and expectation of goodness. He is the only one who can break the chains and walk you into your heart's desires.

Scripture around Freedom from Religious and Poverty Spirits

- Ephesians 2:8–9 (NLT): "God saved you by his grace when you believed. And you can't take credit for this; it is a gift from God. Salvation is not a reward for the good things we have done, so none of us can boast about it."
- 1 John 4:10 (NLT): "This is real love—not that we loved God, but that he loved us and sent his Son as a sacrifice to take away our sins."
- 2 Corinthians 8:9 (ESV): "For you know the grace of our Lord Jesus Christ, that though he was rich, yet for your sake he became poor, so that you by his poverty might become rich."
- Proverbs 6:11 (NIV): "And poverty will come on you like a thief and scarcity like an armed man."

- James 1:17 (MEV): "Every good gift and every perfect gift is from above and comes down from the Father of lights, with whom there is no change or shadow of turning."
- Psalm 51:12 (NKJV): "Restore to me the joy of Your salvation, and uphold me by Your generous Spirit."

Unleash the Box

1. We in the West need to wake up—we are asleep and living in an age of powerless religion. Not everything presented to us is for our good; we must test what we see and hear with Scripture and prayer. How do you decide if something is good and true or if something is false? As my counselor, Kelly, has told me, "Just cause a door opens, it does not mean it is from God."
2. God is a person who speaks into our lives and knowing his voice is part of coming into right relationship with him. Where are you not believing he is a person? What would it take for you to know him as intimately as he wants to be known?
3. We frame our theology by how we relate to God. Typically, we see Father/Yahweh as how we experienced our earthly father,

Holy Spirit as our mom, and Jesus as our siblings and friends. Ask God to highlight your current posture or relation to those earthly relationships in your life. Are there any negative experiences you attribute to God from your earthly experiences? What is true of him and what is not true of him?

4. Consider taking communion every day for seven days. Take water and a cracker or bread; meditate on what it means to take in his body and blood. Picture Christ on the cross who took all our disease, affliction, and sin, and who gave us all of himself. The gift he extends to you is his health, his power, and his freedom. Lay down your life and take up his.

5. The power of the tongue—i.e., the power of our words—can either cause us to speak life or death. What messages are you sending yourself by what you say to yourself? Are you telling yourself you are unique, beautiful, or lovely? Admire the way God made you. As you would do for other people, do for yourself—speak genuine life over yourself and from a true heart. Ask God for the words he speaks over you. What is the Father saying to you now?

6. What barriers do you have in your life that keep you from knowing God more?

7. Is any selfish ambition through building your own life causing a rift in your life with God? Elaborate.

8. Where is the poverty spirit playing a role in your life? Are you believing God can break you free from this mind-set?

9. The less you try to control, the more he will move! Do you believe that? What prevents you from stepping out of the way and surrendering your dreams, desires, and ideas to the One who made you? What does surrender look like to you?

Prayer: Welcome, God; welcome, Jesus; and welcome, Holy Spirit. Welcome to my life. Thank you for tearing down any religious strongholds or poverty spirits at play in your people. Continue to open doors that others have shut. You have big dreams for us. Help us to unearth anything that isn't of you and to fill us with your hope and expectation of goodness. If we show up, you will show off. The less we control, the more you will move! In Jesus's name, amen.

Chapter 10: Finding Freedom and Wholeness in Abundance through Surrender

The more fully you relinquish yourself to Him, the more you will discover that He has your best interests at heart and that His will truly is "good, acceptable, and perfect."

—Nancy DeMoss Wolgemuth

What if surrendering to God is the way to freedom? What if in the surrender we find out not only the purpose to our life, but how to take God out of a box and allow the adventure to begin? It's through the ultimate life surrender we not only become free, but we also become whole. In wholeness we become ourselves. Many Christians reduce their faith to a comfortable set of beliefs about God rather than an adventurous journey where he takes us beyond where we have been.

Do I Really Trust God?

Surrender comes through trust and humility. Faith is the confidence in things unseen. We are confiding in, relying upon, or depending on God. We are to reasonably expect, believe, and entrust ourselves to him. We are to trust in God and his love to provide what we need—both in this life and the next in heaven. Humility is being grounded in the nature of God. Proverbs 3:5 (NIV) commands, "Trust in the LORD with all your heart and lean not on your own understanding." When we commit our ways to the Lord, we trust in God and are often rescued in the process of this trust. When humility is at work in us, we are dependent on grace for all knowing and believing. "In humility receive the word implanted, which is able to save your souls" (James 1:21 NASB). Only through trusting in the Lord can we come into a true understanding of what humility is and how it plays into fully surrendering.

Scripture teaches who God is and how to live out our faith as true. To fully surrender, we must be healed from the lies we have believed and partnerships we've made with the enemy. To run the race of faith and do what God has asked us to do, we must trust and fix our eyes on what God is about and who he is. This often plays out differently in different seasons of our lives as we are each being renewed into a new person. God calls us to walk with him, trusting and surrendering, during each "being" season. We can't walk into this renewal process in our own effort. Renewal and humility are achieved through submitting to the Holy Spirit and recognizing the need to surrender. It is a laying down of everything we have picked up that isn't of him. He wants to heal and strip us of all the schemes of the enemy. This is so we can run light and free with God. To live on earth as Jesus did, we have to walk into this full revelation through relationship. Our relationship with the Lord is more about being than doing. All our doing comes out of who we are. Healing is the work of repairing and restoring areas in our inner world, our sense of who we are, our being.

As your inner world becomes healed, your actions will become fruit borne out of the new inner reality—i.e., "he who began a good work in you will bring it to completion Philippians 1:6 ESV). Your call to "do" something involves seeking him above all else (Matthew 6:33). After doing the hard work of relationship and, as he says in

Matthew 6:33, seeking him first, all else that you need will be added to your life. You will receive every other thing as a by-product added to you if you heed his invitation and promise to seek him first.

During a being season—one in which we focus on simply *being* with the Lord, not on *doing* anything for him—we can come into agreement with him if we choose what God says. To know and hear his voice, we must rightly discern what is and isn't his voice. We are surrounded by so many voices. There are subtle and loud voices, speaking to us about many areas in life, and there are times we take in what they say and give it space, allowing it to influence us without even realizing it. As we hear from God in the same areas, what he says should become a filter to sort out other voices and compare them against the Word of God. What will we receive as truth, as coming from him, and what will we say no to? Scripture says we must take captive all that sets itself against the knowledge of God. There are two parts to this equation. We must rightly know what is of God. Then we must recognize any competing thought, idea, or reality that is seen as trying to assert itself against God and to steal from us. Once we see it for what it is, we can take it captive and say, "Nope, you don't get to stay. I won't entertain you or allow you space in my head, heart, or life."

The next aspect, or stage, of surrender is recognizing that it is a process. God's encouragement is to try not to make the surrender process a to-do as much as an opportunity to *be* in the process with him. As the Bible says, God takes us from glory to glory: "But we all, with open face beholding as in a glass the glory of the Lord, are changed into the same image from glory to glory, even as by the Spirit of the Lord" (2 Corinthians 3:18 KJV). We are to "cease striving and know that [he is] God (Psalm 46:10 NASB1995), lean into him, and respond to however he is leading. We are to talk to him and ask him our questions; we can be honest with him and share with him whatever is in our hearts. He will show us what to do.

As Kelly, my inner healer counselor, once told me in September 2019, "As we walk into healing through trust and humility, what we've known as normal, or our old way of life, becomes replaced by God's way of new life. Increasingly, what we will find and realize is that life as we used to know it will feel heavy and tiring in a way that is no longer what we want to experience as normal." This is true transformation and freedom.

Complete and Utter Surrender

To surrender is to relinquish possession or control of something (i.e., our life, in this case), to let go of our preconceived notions, and to give up or abandon our old ways of living.

Finding freedom and wholeness through surrender leads to abundance. Surrender comes in many forms. For me, surrender came from finding rest in the Lord and letting the Lord fight for me. Exodus 14:14 (NIV) tells us, "The LORD will fight for you; you need only to be still." Each day, can we let go of the need to climb any ladders, fight any battles, or struggle to impress others? Can we simply be still? Our job is to take a deep breath, surrender all situations and people we would like to control, and let God fight for us. Resting and abiding are ways we can actively trust God each day.

Several verses from Exodus 14 were used at a dear friend's funeral. They are verses that speak to the Israelites leaving captivity in Egypt and walking forward before God parts the Red Sea. In verse 13

(NIV), Moses says, "Do not be afraid. Stand firm and you will see the deliverance the LORD will bring you today. The Egyptians you see today you will never see again." In verse 15 (NIV), the Lord says to Moses, "Why are you crying out to me? Tell the Israelites to move on." How often do we exert effort to defend ourselves in battles being waged in our lives when what we really need to do is let God take over? The thing is, the God of the universe has already waged the war on your behalf and claimed the victory over every enemy. All he wants is for you to rest in him and be still. He has got you!

But in our humanness, sometimes we stand there, hearing God say to move on, then telling him, "Awesome, I want to. Just part the sea and then I can go." Our limited understanding of believing means the way must be visible before we obey. But for the Israelites it was taking him at his word and walking in obedience that allowed the waters to part as the sea hit their feet below. So it is with us. We do not want to get ahead of his invitation, or we will drown in the waters and miss his intricately timed details. See, as the Israelites felt the intensity of the earthly reality closing in, Pharoah's army was getting visibly closer. We each have our own version of this earthly tension, circumstances where we need him to make a way. It could have seemed they needed to hurry up and go if they would be able to get away in time. And yet God's delay was a part of his perfect plan, as only because the enemy was that close did they follow the Israelites into the sea, where the sea then closed over the Egyptians. Had the Israelites moved earlier, the enemy might not have been fully destroyed.

This story of God's parting of the Red Sea reminds me that sometimes it is my paradigm that needs to shift. He is healing and stretching my faith. He is not limited to how I see things, to the options I see before me, or to the timing I think his plan must happen in.

Our job is to stay in step with Him. There are times where we might have liked to see the full sea part. Instead he said, "Do this for me," and we stepped forward in obedience even though we didn't see how it was all going to play out and where the full path was before us. But we are trusting the way will open before us as our feet step into the wall of water in obedience to his Word, trusting the One who makes a way where there seems to be no way. And as he did it for the Israelites, so He will do it for each of us. Again and again.

Finding Rest

Stepping into a "being" season means we reorient ourselves to finding true rest in Christ. One of the most powerful verses in the Bible regarding rest, specifically rest for the weary, is Matthew 11:28–30. In the Greek, *anapauo* means "rest." When translated directly, it also means "fresh hope." We can only find this fresh hope as we stop resisting God's truths and start applying them. Let us take a look at a breakdown of this passage and how it relates to finding fresh hope.

Matthew 11:28 (NASB) says, "Come to Me, all who are weary and burdened, and I will give you rest." In my Bible, this verse includes references to other related scriptures elsewhere in the Bible: "If anyone is thirsty, let him come to Me and drink" (John 7:37 NASB); "You there! Everyone who thirsts, come to the waters; And you have no money, come, buy and eat. Come, buy wine and milk without money and without cost" (Isaiah 55:1 NASB); "My presence shall go with you, and I will give you rest" (Exodus 33:14 NASB). Rest was an Old Testament concept that implied secure borders, peace with and absence of threat from neighboring countries, and abundant life and well-being within the land.

Matthew 11:29 (NASB) adds even more significance to the idea of rest: "Take my yoke upon you and learn from me, for I am gentle and humble in heart, and you will find rest for your souls." Other related scriptures are referenced here as well: "For I gave you an example, so that you also would do just as I did for you" (John 13:15 NASB); "Have this attitude in yourselves which was also in Christ Jesus" (Philippians 2:5 NASB); "Chris also suffered for you, leaving you an example, so that you would follow in His steps" (1 Peter 2:21 NASB); "the one who says that he remains in Him ought, himself also, walk just as He walked" (1 John 2:6 NASB).

Finding rest for our souls is also referenced in the following verses of Psalms 116 and Jeremiah 6: "Return to your rest, my soul, for the LORD has been good to you" (Psalms 116:7 NIV); "Stand at the crossroads and look; ask for the ancient paths, ask where the good way is, and walk in it, and you will find rest for your souls" (Jeremiah 6:16 NIV).

Matthew 11:30 (NIV) says, "For my yoke is easy and my burden is light." And according to 1 John 5:3 (NIV), "This is love for God: to obey his commands. And his commands are not burdensome."

Similarly, John 14:15 (NASB) says, "If you love Me, you will keep My commandments." In John 15:10 (NIV) Jesus tells us, "If you keep my commands, you will remain in my love, just as I have kept my Father's commands and remain in his love." Here are some of the commands being referred to: "The LORD is compassionate and gracious, slow to anger, abounding in love" (Psalm 103:8 NIV); "And this is love: that we walk in obedience to his commands. As you have heard from the beginning, his command is that you walk in love" (2 John 6).

The truth is he bears the burdens of life with us. He guides us through this learning process into fresh hope when we find rest. His rest and love are tied together. *Easy* in the Greek means "well-fitting." The yoke of an ox was carefully adjusted so it would fit well, or right. Jesus says his yoke is easy because it represents entering a right relationship with him. His rest is good for our soul. His yoke is easy, and his ways are free and light. In our relationship with God, do we experience unforced rhythms of grace? Do we experience the well-fitting to the truth of who we are created to be? Do we know well the God of Matthew 11:28–30? It is time to taste and see and surrender.

He Giveth

Ephesians 2:6–7 (NIV) says, "And God raised us up with Christ and seated us with him in the heavenly realms in Christ Jesus, in order that in the coming ages he might show the incomparable riches of his grace, expressed in his kindness to us in Christ Jesus."

There may be days when we feel bogged down with stress and struggles over situations in our lives. Perhaps we need a gentle reminder of the Sermon on the Mount where Jesus said, "Seek first his kingdom and his righteousness, and all these things will be given to you as well" (Matthew 6:33 NIV). "All these things" does not include everything we want, but everything we need. To seek the kingdom of God is to seek after God himself, and in earnestly doing so, everything we need becomes everything we want.

God works in us first before he works through us. For most of us, it is in a period of brokenness where we first begin to seek God, and as he puts the pieces of our lives together, he places in our hearts a hunger and thirst to pursue a deeper relationship with him. As we crave his goodness and righteousness more and more, there will come a point when we intentionally turn away from anything we know that is not pleasing to God—a sure sign of the Holy Spirit's work in us.

We can have all the money in the world and still be empty. We can have prestige, power, status, and still not be at peace. We can have it all and lose it all, but when the eyes of our hearts are enlightened by the Holy Spirit, the agenda of Christ takes precedence in our lives. Paul writes, "I pray that the eyes of your heart be enlightened in order that you may know the hope to which he has called you, the riches of his glorious inheritance in his holy people, and his incomparably great power for us who believe" (Ephesians 1:18–19 NIV). In him we find hope, peace, and great riches as the words of this old hymn, "He Giveth More Grace," continue to ring true:

> When we have exhausted our store of endurance
> When our strength has failed ere the day is half done
> When we reach the end of our hoarded resources
> Our Father's full giving has only begun
>
> . . . .
>
> His love has not limits, His grace has no measure

His power no boundary known unto men;

For out of His infinite riches in Jesus

He giveth, and giveth, and giveth again.

No matter what we face, when our eyes are set on God, he gives us every spiritual blessing in Christ (Ephesians 1:3).

The Dreams of Your Future

As you step into surrender, what dreams do you have for your future? It is okay to dream, engage your imagination, and ask the Lord where to go, whom to serve, and how to live abundantly. I recently heard the following quote, which made me think about my dreams for the future: "The dreams of your future have no room for the devastations of your past." God longs to use our life and free us up from our past in order to help us step into our future. When Aaron, Moses's brother, died, the entire house of Israel mourned for him for thirty days (Numbers 20:29). However, after those thirty days, the time of mourning was over, and the Israelites had to move on with life.

There is a great lesson in this: you must push beyond the past to enter the future—a future filled with great things God has planned for you. The apostle Paul knew this, which is why he wrote, "One thing I do: Forgetting what is behind and straining toward what is ahead, I press on toward the goal to win the prize for which God has called me heavenward in Christ Jesus" (Philippians 3:13–14 NIV). You may have great dreams for your future, but if you fill your future with dwelling on junk from your past, then you will never fulfill your dreams. Therefore, like the Israelites, after a certain period you must decide to forget what is behind and press on toward the things that are ahead.

When Moses killed the Egyptian, he wasn't acting out of the purpose God had placed in him; he was acting out of his own impulses instead of relying on God. Dream big with God and let Him fulfill those dreams. We might think, "How can I make this dream happen?" But really we need to surrender and let him work it out for us instead. Instead, we can ask the Lord, "God, could I?" He will overwhelm us—in a good way. When it comes to our future, are we dreaming *with* God? And are we letting him fulfill the desires of our heart because they are in line with his? As you believe Psalm 37:4 (NIV) it reminds us, "Take delight in the LORD, and he will give you the desires of your heart."

From Surrender to Abundance

Only through true surrender of your life can you come into the full abundance the Father has for you. This is the sweet spot, discovering what John 10:10 (NIV) says to be true: "I have come that they may have life, and have it to the full." Do you have life to the full? Do you know what abundance looks like this side of heaven?

"Joy is in the process and strength is the outcome! And because it is God's true nature, there is a place of His joy in us that is constant, regardless of circumstances."[1] Joy is the supernatural delight in God. We will face trials, but joy is our choice! Joy is the gift of his presence, which envelops and protects us. Joy means knowing he is with us on both the good days and the horrible ones. We need to remember that he is good and that he is with us. "A cheerful heart is good medicine, but a broken spirit saps a person's strength" (Proverbs

17:22 NLT). Begin each day in joyful expectation and watch what God does.

In John 10:10 (AMP), we're told, "The thief comes only in order to steal and kill and destroy. I came that they may have and enjoy life, and have it in abundance [to the full, till it overflows]." It is no coincidence that abundant living is tied to understanding how the enemy comes in and tries to steal, kill, and destroy. As believers of Jesus, we see life a little differently. We are free to walk around seeking goodness because that means we are seeking after God. If we follow his teachings and bask in his promises, we can walk about in freedom. As Psalm 119:45 (NIV) says, "I will walk about in freedom, for I have sought out your precepts."

To live life more abundantly means choosing full over empty. Choosing to enjoy our life and the people in it means finding the fun despite any hardship. Finding new ways to enjoy life allows us to show others how joyful we are. We can pray, "God, when circumstances arise that steal my hope, remind me of your goodness. Show me how to live to the full. Help me to fix my eyes on you."

God's heart for us is full restoration in him from glory to glory. He says, "Take my hand and come with me."

Lord, give each of us courage to show up for this process. Give us renewed energy and strength, and for every promise of yours be fulfilled before our natural eyes. Taste abundant life and rest in our hearts more than any other thing. Your goodness, kindness, and faithfulness are tangible; let us count the ways we have tasted and seen him. Lord, cover and surround us with your nearness and presence. Go before us, leading us in paths of peace so we will not know want.

God's desire and commitment are to see us realize the healing, wholeness, freedom, and abundant life that is available to us—if we will only choose to live in him and him alone!

As you enter this process of freedom and wholeness, I would love to know how God has healed you. Send your stories to hello@heathervshore.com. May you taste and see goodness in the land of the living! "Maranatha (O our Lord, come)!" (1 Corinthians 16:22 AMP).

Scripture around Freedom in Abundance through Surrender

- Psalm 91:1–2 (NIV): "Whoever dwells in the shelter of the Most High will rest in the shadow of the Almighty. I will say of the LORD, 'He is my refuge and my fortress, my God, in whom I trust.'"

- Romans 12:1–2 (ESV): "I appeal to you therefore, brothers, by the mercies of God, to present your bodies as a living sacrifice, holy and acceptable to God, which is your spiritual worship. Do not be conformed to this world, but be transformed by the renewal of your mind, that by testing you may discern what is the will of God, what is good and acceptable and perfect."

- Deuteronomy 6:5 (ESV): "You shall love the LORD your God with all your heart and with all your soul and with all your might."

- Isaiah 61:7 (NLT): "Instead of shame and dishonor, you will enjoy a double share of honor. You will possess a double portion of prosperity in your land, and everlasting joy will be yours."

- Isaiah 61:7 (AMP): "Instead of your [former] shame you will have a double portion; And instead of humiliation your people will shout for joy over their portion. Therefore in their land they will possess double [what they had forfeited]; everlasting joy will be theirs."
- Psalm 37:4 (NIV): "Take delight in the LORD, and he will give you the desires of your heart."

Unleash the Box

1. Obedience to God without dependence on him is a burden, but when we unite obedience with dependence, his activity becomes the source of our activity. Where are you not surrendering in obedience to God?
2. What distracts you from joyful obedience? Will you ask God to help you delight in working out his Word and his will in your life today?
3. We hinder the Holy Spirit from working in our lives by compromising truth in our innermost being. When we do not partner with the Holy Spirit in bringing about our wholeness,

we place strongholds or lies in our innermost being. What lies are you believing that are keeping you from surrendering to Christ?

4. As God lays his answers before you, sit, reflect, and ask God about them. Tell him honestly where you wish his answers were different than what he said, or you question his answer. Engage with him where you don't agree. Ask questions. Offer your desires. See how he responds. Get to know yourself, what is true of who you are, who you were created to be, and who you desire to be. There are places in us where we have been conditioned to be who we think we are supposed to be or to outwardly perform according to who we think we are. Does who you are and how you're living align with who God says you are? How can alignment with him lead to trust and humility and surrender?

5. One of the visions given to me during my season of surrender was of Jesus taking the weight I was carrying from me, throwing it off, and then asking me to go swim with him. Water typically represents life in the Spirit. God talks about

people being thirsty and him being the water of life. The vision given was an invitation—to you and to me—to walk with Jesus into what is ahead. Not by our effort, but with Jesus taking the weight from us and inviting us to swim with him into the pool of the Spirit. We will come out feeling refreshed. As we walk into healing through trust and humility, what we've known as normal becomes replaced by God's new way of life. Are you trusting him for your new way of life?

6. Where can you find rest through surrender? In what area, or areas, of life is he calling you to surrender?
7. Can you dream with God about your future? What would those dreams entail? Ask him to break down the barriers keeping your imagination under lock and key.
8. What part of abundance are you not believing Christ for? Ask him to show you. The less you control, the more he will move!

Prayer: Precious Lord, thank you for the glorious riches we have in surrendering our lives to you. We ask that your agenda take precedence in our lives and that we learn to draw on every blessing we have in you. You are our provider, and no ill-fitting thing will be placed on us. Heavenly Father, thank you for the reminder that obedience to you must never be separated from dependence on you. May we experience a deeper realization of your working in and through us. In Jesus's name, amen.

Appendix

My Freedom and Wholeness Journey

My freedom and wholeness journey came from sitting on the back side of the mountain, both literally and figuratively. I hated being there at times, but it taught me to know how to walk closely with our Lord. Providing details of my personal healing journey during Sozo, an inner healing experience, will hopefully give you encouragement to take the leap into your own heart journey. God pursues each of us in mighty and different ways. My hope is for others to experience his supernatural healing.

2017 – Joined leadership at BSF (Bible Study Fellowship) for the Romans study (cried every week as God began undoing all the yuck in my life).

March 2018 – Saw an angel the week before my cancer surgery, which was on March 27, 2018. An angel showed up during my quiet time and so overshadowed me with God's love, I was forever undone.

Last Week of March 2018 – Planned to get my first book, *Deeply Wounded Hope*, translated into Arabic due to the word I received from the Lord during BSF in 2018. My first book encompasses overcoming domestic violence with the help of the Lord.

June 13, 2018 – Received word from Kelly, my inner healing counselor, asking about inner healing with her and citing Matthew 6:33, which would become my verse through this healing season.

October 7, 2018 – Met a prophet at Subway who quoted Matthew 6:33 before feeding some homeless people.

February 19, 2019 – Reconnected with Kelly regarding supernatural healing through email and social media and all God was calling me into, and she used Matthew 6:33 again. God kept asking me to lay everything down and seek Him above all else, and I was very hesitant. He kept using the same verse repeatedly everywhere I went.

April 2019 – Went to Arabic church where God had a direct word for me after the church service about starting a church.

May 2019 – Received from God the download of the table of contents for this book (he woke me up in the middle of the night); told Dale, my previous coach, and Dale said that was very unusual to receive such revelation from him.

June 4, 2019 – Had my first Sozo call with Kelly and the vision of the victory sign from Lana Vawser prophecy (https://lanavawser.com/2019/06/04/i-heard-the-lord-say-my-pioneers-my-forerunners-where-you-have-barely-survived-now-you-will-thrive/) was in my first house exercise.

July 19, 2019 – Vision about the little girl and the trip she is on. This correlated with the original vision of me getting into a wagon and letting Jesus take me (pull me) where I needed to go. During the vision, he gave me Matthew 6:33. Every time I moved off the path, he reminded me of the wagon.

August 12, 2019 – Heard from God that he brought me back to Colorado to heal me, that I would be released.

September 4–October 18, 2019 – Trinity Bible Study started with Kelly and Tina; during this time, I was watching the *Sheep Among Wolves* documentary on the women in Iran, when God told me the women in Iran are one of the reasons, I went through abuse (my story is detailed in *Deeply Wounded Hope*) and asked me to lay down my life for him.

October 1, 2019 – Finished Arabic version of my first book, *Deeply Wounded Hope*.

October 10, 2019 – Began fulfilling speaking engagements based on Deeply Wounded Hope.

October 22, 2019 – Experienced significant healing session with Kelly where three demonic spirits left my house (inner being) and God gave my life back in a blue box.

January 2020 – Received prayer and note from Kelly via email:

> *Father, would you give Heather glimpses of her land? Bring her tastes and visions of the goodness that awaits her in the land of the living and fill her with renewed strength and energy that leads to increased belief and persevering endurance. Thank you that you promise to see her through to the end, as she simply will not give up. In Jesus's name, amen.*
>
> Ask God to reveal what he knows is here. What things would fill in this blank in your true heart: I will

radically obey, no matter what you ask, so long as_____?

What are the unspoken (and possibly unconscious) parameters and limitations you're holding God to around what you will do, what he can ask you, what sacrifice or cost it can require?

2020 – The year my divorce started. There are too many miracles to count of God's goodness and provision through this. Where he will take me and my children remains to be seen, but he has shown up in numerous ways, all the while displaying his goodness and mercy for us.

Broken Record Prophecy

Dennis Funderberg is a pastor and prophet in Texas and his podcast, *Jesus Is Still Jesus,* has touched the lives of thousands. Below is a prophecy which rocked my world as I started to step into my identity in Christ:

Beloved, I'm calling you higher for you to see in fullness who I called you to be, and I call you deep.

Deeper into the depths of who I am, pure revelation and insight. Beloved, I want you to know more of who I am and what I want to do in your life, in this current time. I am not bound by the restrictions of the world; they can try all they want but they can never restrict the Great I Am. My pursuit of you is everlasting. I will pursue you always. The day we joined in union face-to-fact, you and I will enjoy each other for all of eternity. I am not hindered by what you're struggling with or anxious about the day ahead. I am still on my throne and I am still in control. I am not alarmed by those who despise me, I am not frantic by those who think they can overcome me. I laugh at those who thing they can bring destruction onto the church; I will have my way. But will you let me have my way in your life? A part of my heart is gentle which means I am also patient. I will wait . . . I will wait for when you say yes you can have this area of my life. I will not intrude, but I will knock. I will keep knocking . . . The deepest hurts of your life beloved are not the areas I want to avoid; they are the areas I want to up right into the middle. The doubts you have I want to replace with faith, the hurts you have I want to bring healing. Want to turn grief into joy beloved. I want to show up in your life in amazing and marvelous ways, but you gotta let me in. I am everything you have hoped I would be and even more. I want to help you, I want to hold you and want to provide for you. I don't ever want you to be afraid. If you are ever to look in the mirror, I want you to see me staring back at you. Sweetheart, people in the world said you were nothing, but to me you are worth it. Son, for those who said you couldn't, who said you never would be, and the times you've tried to do it in your own strength and tried to prove them wrong, I am here for you. For those that are tired, trust me, lean on me. For those who are panicked for the future ahead, I am in control. I know what tomorrow holds, and I know what I want to do in your life. For those who face betrayal, let me kiss you. Let me kiss the area of your life that have been so dark and so burdened, let me in. Just know when you let me into those sensitive areas of your life, I am not going to condemn you, or shake my finger in your face and tell you how you missed it. No that is not my heart at all! If you let me in, I will show you who I really call you to be and how those inconsistencies are not what I wanted for you. It's not what I wanted but I will change it. Beloved I want you. I want you. For those who have felt they could never be wanted, I want you.[1]

Pocket Prayers on Friendship from Max Lucado

When we need the words to pray for our relationships and friends, here are some wonderful prayers to remind us of the gift of friendships:

Pocket Prayer 1: Almighty God, Help me to reflect your love and embrace the wisdom you offer. I ask you to bring healthy friendships into my life and to protect me from relationships that would pull me away from you. Bring positive influences into the lives of my friends. Equip them to sharpen each other to become more like you every day. Thank you for caring about every aspect of my life, especially the people in it. And you for continuing to open doors to relationships that honor you. Amen.

Pocket Prayer 2: Heavenly Father, I praise you for your constant involvement in my life. You never fail to meet all my needs and to lead me in truth. I need discernment today regarding the friendships I allow in my life. Give me wisdom to know which relationships to embrace and which ones to pass by. I ask you to guide my friends in this too. Protect them from negative influences that might draw them away from your presence. Thank you for being a constant friend. Every in temporary season of loneliness, you're with me. I'm so grateful for your presence when other relationships are in transition. In Jesus's name, amen.

Pocket Prayer 3: Almighty God, you are a constant in my life. I praise you for your faithfulness. Even if everyone around me fails, you never do. I can always count on your presence. Equip me to trust you in new ways and to greater depths. Help me release any fears I'm carrying and remind me that you have never left me and will never forsake me. In turn, I want to be someone my friends can always trust and depend on.

Bless my friends with your presence when they struggle with loneliness. Be the companion they seek. Pursue their hearts, and reassure them that they are never alone, because you are always there. Thank you for the gift of your constant presence. Thank you for joy of friendship and the companionship it brings. In the powerful name of Jesus, amen.

Pocket Prayer 4: Dear Father God, I praise you for your plan for my life. You are the God of the entire universe, yet you are so good to me and are involved in the details of my day. Help me trust you with my day and every detail in it so I will walk with you and not go down my own path. I want my steps to be ordered by you so my mind will be at ease.

Help my friends trust that you are at work in their lives too. I pray that they will strive to honor you with every part of their day. As they commit their steps to you, give them peace and sureness of mind. Provide them with clarity so they do not have to wander aimlessly but instead will live with purpose. Thank you for giving me friends who walk with me on this path through life. I look forward to every celebration and joyous moment to be shared. In Jesus's name, Amen.

Prayer for Breaking Generational Curses

Below is an extensive series of prayers you can pray to break curses that have existed among your family for generations:

First, take the time to read all of Deuteronomy 28.

Second, make sure you don't have any bitterness toward others, self or God. Otherwise, the prayer will not work. We are commanded to forgive those who hurt us and pray for them.

Third say the prayer out loud:

Thank you that your blood is able to take away all sin. I believe that and receive it now in Jesus' name.

I pray forgiveness for the sins of my father, of that bloodline for all generations back, and I ask You to wash me clean now, by the blood of the Lamb. I pray forgiveness for the sins of my mother, of that bloodline for all generations back, and I ask You to wash me clean now, by the blood of the Lamb. I receive Your forgiveness and believe that by Your blood I am cleansed from the sins of all my generational bloodlines.

I take the authority that I have in my blood covenant with Jesus Christ, and I break all generational curses on my father's side all generations back, broken now, by the blood of the Lamb.

I take that same authority and break all generational curses on my mother's side, all generations back, broken now, by the blood of the Lamb.

With the same authority I have under the blood covenant of salvation in Jesus, I break any spoken curses on my family bloodline. I also break the power of all seals of silence and all vows of secrecy. I take the same authority in the name and the blood of Jesus, and I break all covenants and contracts to Satan including blood covenant contracts.

I also pray forgiveness for the sins of my family line of all those things that have happened in darkness, such as any attachment to slavery or any kind of persecution or mistreatment or abuse of any people groups or individuals, and I pray blessings on all descendants of the persecuted groups or individuals. I also break any attachments to family superstitions and idolatries, ungodly beliefs, wives tales, luck charms, and rhyme curses in Jesus' name.

Thank you, Jesus, that Your word says, "Cursed is the one who hangs on the tree." You took our curses, and You took our sins, so that we can have life more abundantly, and we praise you for it.

I receive by faith that now all generational sins and all generational curses are broken by the blood of the Lamb, in Jesus's name. Amen.[2]

Notes

Chapter 1

1 Oral Roberts, *If You Need Healing, Do These Things* (City: Oral Roberts, 1969), Page 5.
2 Stormie Omartian, *Lord, I Want to Be Whole: The Power of Prayer and Scripture in Emotional Healing* (Nashville: Thomas Nelson, 2000), Page 7.
3 Michael Jake, "The Backside of the Desert: A Sermon on Moses," published June 15, 2014, https://www.sermoncentral.com/sermons/the-backside-of-the-desert-michael-jakes-sermon-on-moses-185979.
4 Joyce Simmons, "On the Back Side of the Desert," *Charisma Leader Magazine*, June 30, 2000, https://ministrytodaymag.com/leadership/ethics/423-on-the-back-side-of-the-desert.
5 Nancy Missler, "Reflections of His Image: Where Does Self Life Come From?" Koinonia House, khouse.org, October 1, 2007, https://www.khouse.org/articles/2007/739/.

Chapter 2

2 Bible Study Fellowship, Acts and Letters of Apostles Study, James 3-5, Lesson 29
2 Joseph Mattera, "Ten Signs You Have a Religious Spirit," August 6th, 2017, https://josephmattera.org/ten-signs-you-have-a-religious-spirit/
3 Alyssa J. Howard, "Your Inheritance in Christ: What Does It Mean to Be an Heir?" published October 17th, 2018, https://www.alyssajhoward.com/2018/10/17/inheritance-in-christ/

Chapter 3

1 Lana Vawser, "I Heart the Lord say a Tidal Wave of My Love is Crashing into the Hidden Prisons of Self-hatred Many of My Daughters are Caught in and I am Setting Them Free Bringing Healing Freedom and a Fresh Revelation of My Love, Their Identity in Me and Purpose," March 3, 2019, https://lanavawser.com/2019/03/18/i-heard-the-lord-say-a-tidal-wave-of-my-love-is-crashing-into-the-hidden-prisons-of-self-hatred-many-of-my-daughters-are-caught-in-and-i-am-setting-them-free-bringing-healing-freedom-and-a-fresh-r/.
2 "What Are Evidences of Self-Rejection?" Institute in Basic Life Principles, www.iblp.org, accessed January 27, 2022, https://iblp.org/questions/what-are-evidences-self-rejection.
3 Charles Stanley, "Self-Rejection: Its Characteristics, Causes & Cures," radio message, January 1990,

https://mylifewithlymphedema.blogspot.com/2005/10/lymphedema-and-your-self-image.html.
4 Charles Stanley, "Self-Rejection: Its Characteristics, Causes & Cures."
5 Kim Dolan Leto, Strong, Confident, His, episode 61, "The First Step to Get Fit, Healthy and Whole in Christ.".

Chapter 4
1 Marti Pieper, "John Wimber's First Healing Miracle Shows Why We Still Need the Holy Spirit," CharismaNews.com, August 16, 2021, https://www.charismanews.com/marketplace/86421-john-wimber-s-first-healing-miracle-shows-why-we-still-need-the-holy-spirit.

Chapter 5
1 Henry Cloud, *Necessary Endings: The Employees, Businesses, and Relationships That All of Us Have to Give Up in Order to Move Forward,* (New York: Harper Business, 2010), page 142.
2 Tom Rath, *Vital Friends: The People You Can't Afford to Live Without* (New York: Gallop Press, 2006), page 76.
3 Dr. Henry Cloud, *Necessary Endings: The Employees, Businesses, and Relationships That All of Us Have to Give Up in Order to Move Forward* (New York: Harper Business, 2010), page 7.
4 Bob Goff and Lewis Howes, School of Greatness podcast.

Chapter 6
1 Lonnie Nix, "Sowing and Reaping in the Kingdom," sermon, published online May 5, 2017, https://thewaytribe.com/sowing-and-reaping-in-the-kingdom/.

Chapter 7
1 Lisa Terkeurst, *Made to Crave* (Grand Rapids, MI: Zondervan, 2010), page 121.
2 "Prayer to Renounce Generational Family Iniquity," TruthinReality.com, August 3, 2012, https://truthinreality.com/2012/08/03/prayers-renouncing-generational-family-iniquity/.

Chapter 8
1 Jamie Rohrbaugh, "11 Prophetic Words for 2021," FromHisPresence.com, January 14, 2021, https://www.fromhispresence.com/11-prophetic-words-for-2021/.
2 Jamie Rohrbaugh, "11 Prophetic Words for 2021."

Chapter 9
1 For more explanation of these concepts, go to SozoGroup.com.
2 Dennis Funderberg, "Victory from the Poverty Spirit," *Jesus Is Still Jesus* podcast, episode 25, https://podcasts.apple.com/us/podcast/victory-from-the-spirit-of-poverty-ep-25/id1472556919?i=1000467530239.

Chapter 10
1 Graham Cooke, "How Best to Travel with God," BrilliantPerspectives.com, August 13, 2018, https://brilliantperspectives.com/how-best-to-travel-with-god/.

Appendix
1 Dennis Funderberg, "Broken Record Prophecy," *Jesus Is Still Jesus* podcast, episode 42, December 30th, 2020.
2 "Breaking Generational or Inherited Iniquity Means Breaking Strongholds of the Mind – Wrong Thinking," accessed September 1, 2021, https://healingdeliverance.net/what-exactly-is-inherited-iniquity-p2/.

www.ingramcontent.com/pod-product-compliance
Lightning Source LLC
Chambersburg PA
CBHW051428290426
44109CB00016B/1469